CENTERBROOK

VOLUME 2

ANDREA OPPENHEIMER DEAN

Foreword by Vincent J. Scully, Jr.
Afterword by Nicholas Negroponte

ROCKPORT PUBLISHERS

ROCKPORT, MASSACHUSETTS

First published in the United States of America by:
Rockport Publishers, Inc.
146 Granite Street
Rockport, Massachusetts 01966-1299
Telephone: (508) 546-9590
Fax: (508) 546-7141

Distributed to the book trade and art trade in the United States by:
AIA Press
1735 New York Avenue NW
Washington, DC 20006
(800) 365-2724

Other Distribution by:
Rockport Publishers
Rockport, Massachusetts 01966-1299

ISBN 1-56496-235-0

10 9 8 7 6 5 4 3 2 1

Design: Dutton & Sherman Design
Cover Photographs *(all except bottom left)*: Jeff Goldberg/Esto
(bottom left): Robert Benson

Printed in Hong Kong by Regent Publishing Services Limited

CONTENTS

4

ACKNOWLEDGMENTS

5

FOREWORD

Vincent Scully

6

INTRODUCTION

Andrea Oppenheimer Dean

BUILDINGS AND PROJECTS

202

AFTERWORD

Nicholas Negroponte

203

PROJECT CREDITS

208

AUTHOR AND CONTRIBUTORS

Acknowledgments

I would like to thank Vincent Scully and Nicholas Negroponte for their written contributions; the partners of Centerbrook for giving freely of their time and thoughts; and the clients of Centerbrook for permitting publication of the projects.

Photography makes up a vital part of this book, and I would like to give special recognition to the superb work of photographers Jeff Goldberg of Esto, Steve Rosenthal, Robert Benson, Norman McGrath, Timothy Hursley, Brian Vanden Brink, and Langdon Clay.

The staff at Centerbrook has contributed immeasurably to the assembly of the book, and I would like to express my special appreciation to Margaret Wazuka and Matt Conley for their invaluable assistance. I would also like to recognize Genie Devine, Leslie Henebry, and Nancy King for their support in completing the manuscript, and David Huggins, John Doyle, Mike Garner, Steve Tiezzi, Greg Nucci, and Stephen Laput for their assistance in producing most of the drawings for the book.

My sincere appreciation goes to Rosalie Grattaroti, Don Fluckinger, Barbara States, Lynne Havighurst, and Kathy Kelley at Rockport Publishers for their guidance and design.

Andrea Oppenheimer Dean

*F*OREWORD

It seems to me that Centerbrook's work gets better every year. Like that of a number of architecture firms today, it exemplifies in large part the revival of the vernacular classical tradition that has been going on for the past thirty years or so, but it has a special, loose-jointed flair of its own.

Some of its quality derives from Centerbrook's relation to the late and sorely missed Charles Moore. That incomparably intelligent and profoundly civilized architect was a major instigating force of the vernacular and classical renewal. It was he more than anyone else who let the air out of High Modernism's often gloomy pretensions and brought humor back into architecture, along with all kinds of eclectic variety and playfulness of form. Moreover, Moore was a kind of perennial nomad, wandering around the country as if without a fixed abode.

Everywhere he went he attracted young architects to his low-keyed crusade, and firm after firm of them sprang up around him from Austin to Los Angeles, and not least in Centerbrook's Connecticut itself, where the firm was founded by students of Moore's at Yale. Here Mark Simon, Jeff Riley, Chad Floyd, Bill Grover, Bob Harper, and Jim Childress develop their work in ways that do him honor: from delightful furniture, often wonderfully zany, to happily conceived residences of all kinds and, increasingly, to highly sympathetic institutional buildings.

ABOVE: Quinnipiac College Lender School of Business Center's landmark globe complements the building's setting against the Sleeping Giant Mountain.
Photo: Jeff Goldberg/Esto

I have been happy to follow the course of their work at Quinnipiac College, whose campus lies not far north of my home in New Haven, directly under the grand long body of the mountain called "The Sleeping Giant." It was upsetting to watch earlier buildings at the college rise on that splendid site without much distinction of detail or general order, but as soon as Centerbrook took over everything changed. Centerbrook's Law and Business schools at Quinnipiac have gone far toward relating the campus to the mountain with tact and dignity. The organization of the site as a whole looks better every day, and the buildings themselves have become ever more solid in detail and massing and increasingly worthy of their noble situation under the mountain mass.

At Quinnipiac, Centerbrook has done the best thing that architects can do anywhere. It has made a place where the natural and the manmade supplement each other in quiet grandeur. It is a mythic setting, the Sleeping Giant, a sacred mountain where the citizens of New Haven once sent their women and children for refuge when the British invaded the city during the Revolution. I remember walking and climbing there with a profound sense of coming home after the Second World War.

If Centerbrook's architects had never done anything else, they would have to be remembered for saving this place. But such is not the case. They have gone on to meet many other challenges, armed with Moore's precious legacy of wit and forbearance, and with their own version of his gentle, loving eye.

Vincent J. Scully, Jr.
New Haven, Connecticut

*I*NTRODUCTION

Andrea Oppenheimer Dean

Since publication of Rockport's first book about Centerbrook in 1993, the firm has completed more than 60 design projects ranging from house additions to complex institutional, industrial, and technical buildings and master plans. Centerbrook's recent commissions have tended to become larger in size, more complicated in scope, and more confident and sophisticated in execution. And the firm has extended its reach beyond New England into the South, the Middle West, and the Rockies.

The partners, all of whom are designers, are now in their 40s and 50s and nearing their most creative potential. They have shaped Centerbrook into a practice of more than 60 employees. Perhaps most striking, however, is that increasingly they have fashioned Centerbrook into a peculiarly American architectural firm. And what better context for such a phenomenon than the small, traditional town of Essex, Connecticut?

The firm's six partners share a bracing American optimism. No dark, brooding European *weltschmerz* for them. They take delight in the potential of a building to be fanciful and thereby lighten the angst of everyday life. And they are convinced that profound or brilliant design begins not with moralistic ideologies, abstract theories, or trend-driven stylistic formulas. Transcendent architecture, they believe, starts with fulfilling elemental human needs, with "trying to make an uplifting place out of the particular situation and budget available to us," says partner Bill Grover.

LEFT: The six partners and 12 associates of Centerbrook pose by the waterfall that generates the electricity for their mill building offices.
Upper row, standing (Left to Right): Chad Floyd, Jeff Riley, Jim Childress, Sue Wyeth, Matt Conley, Jim Martin, Mahdad Saniee, Dennis Dowd, Ida Vorum, Charles Mueller.
Middle row (Left to Right): Mark Simon, Bob Harper, Jim Coan, Jean Smajstrla.
Lower row, standing (Left to Right): Bill Grover, Trip Wyeth, Nick Deaver, Walker Burns.
Photo:
Jeanette Montgomery Barron

Grover and each of his five partners—Bob Harper, Jeff Riley, Mark Simon, Chad Floyd, and Jim Childress—can be described by such typically Yankee characteristics as pragmatism, efficiency, and resourcefulness. As a result they cheerfully extract inspiration from an abundance of sources, with the aim of embodying in their buildings the requirements and aspirations of their clients. Also typically New World is their eagerness to be inventive in solving design problems—as evidenced, for example, by Riley's use of boat construction methods to build the domes of the Quinnipiac Law School, in Hamden, Connecticut, or Childress's use of a sandwich made of rice paper between glass-paneled doors to create a sturdier form of shoji screen in a house for a Japanese-American client in Guilford, Connecticut. And in the tradition of America's maverick genius, Frank Lloyd Wright, Centerbrook's designers have embraced craftsmanship as a principal means of enriching their work. "The evidence," notes Harper, "is apparent in the firm's predilection for imaginatively and carefully wrought detailing and its custom-designed outdoor and indoor furniture and fixtures, including fountains, benches, light fixtures, murals, mosaics, wallpapers, carpets, and fireplace utensils."

Unlike Wright's working methods, however, which tended toward the patriarchal and autocratic, "Centerbrook's approach is easy-going and democratic," stresses Floyd. "We do not dictate to clients or to anyone else. We listen, we discuss, and we compromise

ABOVE LEFT: This waterfront house for the director of the Cold Spring Harbor Laboratory takes its inspiration from Sir John Soane's Regency architecture in London, as well as from its Victorian neighborhood.
Photo: Jeff Goldberg/Esto

ABOVE RIGHT: Copper-fritted composite domes with clear acrylic inserts at the Quinnipiac College School of Law Center use advanced boat construction technology.
Photo: Jeff Goldberg/Esto

LEFT: The 1995 "Fashion Show" party, the latest annual extravaganza produced by the employees of Centerbrook in which guests provide the entertainment.
Photo: Jeff Goldberg/Esto

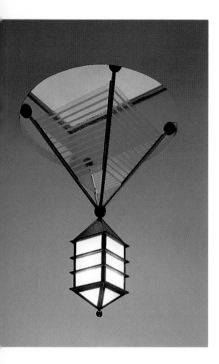

ABOVE: This Centerbrook-designed light fixture softens the daylight from above.
Photo: Jeff Goldberg/Esto

RIGHT: Custom designed railings, moldings, doors, and windows show Centerbrook's attention to craft.
Photo: Jeff Goldberg/Esto

in a thousand ways to make our buildings work," adds Simon. The firm's high percentage of repeat clients would indicate that its methods are effective.

Centerbrook's democratic approach has prompted it to adapt to design the former House Speaker "Tip" O'Neill's admonition that "all politics is local." For Centerbrook, all architecture is local because it responds to local problems and situations and requires tailor-made solutions. In fact, argue the partners, the more particular the solutions, the richer the results. "As the neighborhoods of America are wonderfully diverse, so too, we hope, will be our buildings," says Floyd.

Centerbrook's overriding aim, in short, is to arrive, through democratic methods, at design solutions that appear to be unmistakably appropriate or, in the partners' words, "genuine," because they respond directly to particular circumstances, fulfill emotional and intellectual needs, and express the culture of the locale and the client. Among Centerbrook's tools are the use of vernacular references, local building materials, pertinent symbols,

an understanding of what Riley calls "human sociability," and craftsmanship.

The design process often begins with democratically conducted design workshops resembling New England town meetings. The workshops are aimed at revealing the wishes and preferences of users and community groups and at identifying the spirit of the project's site or locale. "The process makes us become mediums of the culture," says Riley. If the architects are mediums, their buildings are messages that, through a rare combination of flair and reserve, enrich our lives.

Centerbrook's history, too, is an American success story. The practice was founded as Moore Grover Harper in 1975 by Bill Grover, Bob Harper, Jeff Riley, and the peripatetic Charles Moore, who was destined to move on to California the same year. Mark Simon and Chad Floyd soon joined the firm, and in 1984 the partners renamed it for the village in which its offices are located. Since its beginnings the practice has been defined and developed by the five men who as young partners helped Moore found the firm and have stayed with it ever since. In 1996, they expanded the partnership to include Childress, a longtime associate.

Perhaps the most arresting aspect of Centerbrook's recent work is its broad stylistic diversity. This is largely a result of the partners' desire to reflect local culture and conditions in all their rich variety, as is evident, for example, in Floyd's recent, very Floridian expansion scheme for the Norton Museum of Art in West Palm Beach, Florida. There are striking differences in design signatures not only among the Centerbrook designers but also among various buildings by the same designer.

For example, look at two contrasting designs by Simon: a house on the Connecticut shore and the National Maritime Center in Norfolk, Virginia. The Connecticut residence is a contemporary version of a Victorian Gothic-style house, whose forms, while striking, blend with those of neighboring Stick and Shingle-style houses and seem to grow from the craggy site. The National Maritime Center on Norfolk's waterfront, meanwhile, appears as a supersized hybrid of organic and technology-based shapes resembling a beached leviathan.

The diverse talents of Centerbrook's designers and their insistence on design independence from each other have created an unusual partnership. Riley describes it as one of "stimulation, rather than collaboration, in design."

ABOVE LEFT: Members of the Quinnipiac College community participate in one of Centerbrook's on-site design workshops.
Photo: Leonard J. Wyeth

ABOVE CENTER: Partners and associates gather at a retreat in northern Maine in 1988.
Photo: Chad Floyd

ABOVE RIGHT: The Norton Art Museum reflects its local Floridian culture.
Photo: Kenneth Champlin

THIS PAGE, CLOCKWISE FROM TOP: Centerbrook in its open office setting.
Photo: Chad Floyd

The National Maritime Center by Mark Simon incorporates images of ships and sea creatures.
Photo: Jeff Goldberg/Esto

The Guyott house, also by Simon, combines Victorian, Gothic, and Shingle vernaculars into a contemporary design.
Photo: Jeff Goldberg/Esto

Despite that independence, however, the partners naturally exert a strong design influence on each other. They work in unpartitioned office spaces where everything is open to view, and while they engage in a gentle form of competition, they borrow from each others' and from their employees' bag of inventions and details. "We've grown up together, so what we are is what we've made each other," asserts Simon.

As different as the partners' work may be, all of Centerbrook's buildings share a thoroughgoing contextualism or "situationism," as Floyd calls it. When the partners use the word "context," they mean it to include not only the scale, proportions, materials, and sometimes the style of neighboring buildings, but almost every other variable of a design project—its climate; its site; the culture of its locale; the needs, wishes, and culture of the

client; and the requirements and restrictions imposed by the township, the neighborhood, the neighbors, the surrounding landscape, the budget, and the schedule.

Centerbrook's overriding emphasis on context, in its broadest sense, suggests a number of questions: Is context, even when very loosely defined, a sufficiently strong underlying concept for design? How does a dyed-in-the-wool contextualist respond to a context with few, if any, redeeming qualities? And isn't contextualism innately conservative and restricting? Simon refutes such criticism by saying, "You have to find a way to make sure that your design makes everything around it look better." That includes fast-food establishments, big-box discount retailers, and other formulaic buildings. Floyd elaborates: "Contextual design means using the art of proportion and shape and form to not just fit into the status quo but to elevate it, to provide a direction for a better future." That requires each design to begin with a defining idea that includes but also surpasses the needs of context.

In fact, designing for chaotic or shoddy contexts is one of Centerbrook's strongest suits. "We delight in transforming a place," says Floyd, who used urban design principles to transfigure a former bottleneck of trucks, cars, railroad tank cars, and pedestrians at the Pfizer Pharmaceutical plant into a clean-cut and welcoming entryway and parking facility.

Similarly, at Brandeis University, Simon turned a utilitarian building from the 1950s into an attractive structure

ABOVE: The new entry gate helps bring the aging Pfizer Pharmaceutical plant into the 21st century.
Photo: Jeff Goldberg/Esto

RIGHT: A swanlike entry canopy and rooftop sign transform the Brandeis University admissions building into an attraction.
Photo: Steve Rosenthal

by adding a swan-like entrance canopy. And for Quinnipiac College in Hamden, Connecticut, Riley transformed a haphazard assemblage of mediocre buildings into a cohesive and dignified—yet informal—campus.

Another characteristic that unites Centerbrook's buildings is that almost all go to great lengths to provide ample, often unexpected opportunities for people to casually come together and socialize—a not inconsiderable contribution at a time when most societal forces, and especially computerization, are encouraging ever-increasing isolation. In each of Riley's several design projects for Quinnipiac College, for example, he has created a variety of casual, cozy, and inventive meeting places for what he calls "sociability." Outdoors, he has carved out places to sit along meandering paths, on campus stairs, and in specially designed suntraps. Indoors, Riley has similarly scooped out spaces, outside classrooms and along corridors, where small groups can continue their classroom work or simply socialize.

As Centerbrook's partners extend their cooperative independence into a third decade of working together, they are pointedly simplifying their designs and more ruthlessly editing their ideas. Among several examples are two recently completed buildings by Grover. One is a laboratory, office building, and greenhouse for the DeKalb Genetics Corporation in Stonington, Connecticut, a small complex that is made up of elemental, barn-like shapes to reflect the rural site and the agrarian origins of DeKalb. Grover's design for the Pall Corporation Technical Center on Long Island, meanwhile, is also made up of simple shapes, albeit sleek and high-tech ones, to mirror the materials produced by the company.

BELOW LEFT: The Quinnipiac College campus, built in the early 1960s, is rejuvenated by a series of Centerbrook buildings.
Photo: Jeff Goldberg/Esto

BELOW RIGHT: Places to sit and watch the world go by attract students to the courtyard of the Quinnipiac College School of Law Center.
Photo: Jeff Goldberg/Esto

ABOVE: The simplified shapes of the Discovery Research Center at DeKalb Plant Genetics Corporation and the Pall Corporation Technical Center indicate one of the directions Centerbrook's work is taking.
Photo (left): Jeff Goldberg/Esto
Photo (right): Robert Benson

BELOW LEFT: Childress' Erle House makes subtle references to traditional Japanese construction and musical notations.
Photo: Jeff Goldberg/Esto

BELOW RIGHT: The main gate at the Pfizer Pharmaceutical plant is an abstraction of industrial images.
Photo: Jeff Goldberg/Esto

Of the firm's future course, Childress, Centerbrook's newest partner, senses "an interest in being more subtle in how our work fits a context. Harper's historic imagery often has some twist or invention that answers to a particular client's whim or quirk of the site. But I also see an interest in bolder, stripped-down shapes and colors (Grover's work), in motion and movement (Simon's work), in sociability (Riley's work), and in abstract technology and the play of symmetry against asymmetries (Floyd's work)."

Grover, who is the eldest of the five and considered by his partners as the glue that has held them together, quips, "A lot of what we've done is a good base. We're ready to get started."

Andrea Oppenheimer Dean

Wilson Hall

Dartmouth College
Hanover, New Hampshire

The renovation of the three-story Wilson Hall at Dartmouth College transforms a circa 1884 Richardsonian library from an underutilized multi-purpose building into a needed performing arts facility. Centerbrook faithfully restored Wilson Hall's exterior but created new interior elements that sharply contrast with the architecture of the historic building.

The upper floors contain Dartmouth's film studies department and studios, along with rehearsal space for the adjacent Hopkins Center for Performing Arts. The middle floor provides seminar and lecture rooms, and houses the drama department's library. The basement's tangle of Romanesque brick arches houses administrative offices for the Hopkins Center.

The building is attached to the Hood Museum of Art by a new connector that extends Wilson's basement and middle levels into the Hopkins Center lobby.

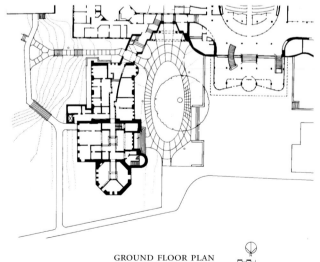

GROUND FLOOR PLAN

OPPOSITE: Centerbrook restored the exterior of Wilson Hall, painting the window trim black to brighten up the contrasting red brick.
Photo: Timothy Hursley

LEFT: A mysterious room in the shape of a green cylinder, centered on the building's restored entry doors, contains a seminar room and the drama department's library.
Photo: Steve Rosenthal

BELOW: Wilson Hall's former coal-storage basement has been converted into administrative offices for the Hopkins Center for the Performing Arts.
Photo: Steve Rosenthal

ENTRY PLAN

UPPER FLOOR PLAN

*H*ouse in Rural Connecticut

This house for a couple and their two children claims the high ground of a site overlooking rolling hills and horse pastures in northwestern Connecticut. The clients, who are equestrians, wanted a house that captured the spirit of the relaxed country houses in the area, dramatized the exceptional site, and reflected the personality of the family.

A carefully planned procession begins at the entry gateway, from which different views unfold like pictures in a storybook. A small garden courtyard collects the sun's warmth and the scent of flowers. Inside, an arcaded entry hall receives guests and frames views of the expansive living room beyond. At the focal point of the living room is a fireplace made of stone quarried in Jerusalem and decorated with two mosaics made at a kibbutz in northern Israel. This centerpiece symbolizes the owners' focus on family and religion. A corner of the living area accommodates a grand piano and captures peaceful views of the outdoors. Directly off the kitchen is a large, screen-enclosed porch that allows informal outdoor dining overlooking gardens and a horse barn and paddock.

The second-floor children's rooms form a small house within the house. Interior windows overlook the entry hall and living room, symbolizing both the children's independence and inclusion in family life.

Centerbrook's overall accomplishment was to create a sense of leaving one world and entering another unexpected, personal, and memorable one.

ABOVE: The house commands views of pastures from its hilltop site.
Photo: Norman McGrath

OPPOSITE: The fireplace, made of Jerusalem stone and Israeli mosaics, is the centerpiece of the living room.
Photo: Norman McGrath

SITE PLAN

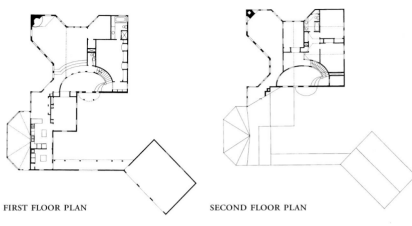

FIRST FLOOR PLAN   SECOND FLOOR PLAN

OPPOSITE, TOP: A covered walk-way connecting the kitchen and garage (right) creates the entry gateway.
Photo: Norman McGrath

OPPOSITE, BOTTOM: Fanciful bookshelves reveal the playful spirit of the owners.
Photo: Norman McGrath

ABOVE: The sun's warmth and garden smells collected in the courtyard create a special ambience along the entry path.
Photo: Norman McGrath

LEFT: The entry hall opens up views into the living room.
Photo: Norman McGrath

Recreation Center

This economical addition to the college's gymnasium makes use of existing stairways, corridors, and locker rooms. On the first floor, a weight room and aerobic exercise room have views of both the outdoors and the activities taking place in the large field house. The field house offers multiple-use courts and a jogging track and frequently accommodates large special events. Daylight from translucent wall panels reduces the need for electric lighting and adds a cheerful atmosphere to this voluminous room. The translucent wall panels also give a soothing quality of light to the two second-floor dance studios, where sophisticated audiovisual equipment is available to students. Interior window walls heighten the awareness of people and activity throughout the complex, making it one of the main social centers on campus.

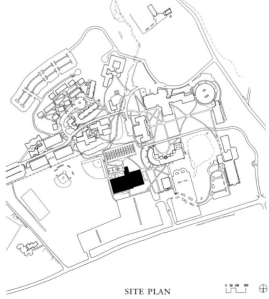

SITE PLAN

FIRST FLOOR PLAN

SECOND FLOOR PLAN

OPPOSITE: The addition creates a secondary public entrance for special events.

Photo: Jeff Goldberg/Esto

ABOVE: Activities are visible throughout the complex, which is now one of the main social centers on campus.

Photo: Jeff Goldberg/Esto

LEFT: Translucent wall panels illuminate both the field house and exercise rooms.

Photo: Jeff Goldberg/Esto

*P*rivate Residence

ABOVE: The new chimney is a visible version of the huge masonry masses that are hidden at the center of colonial houses. The post-and-beam structure is independent of outside walls.
Photo: Chad Floyd

OPPOSITE: The site is a mature New England landscape, tended for 250 years.
Photo: Cervin Robinson

The clients' requirements were to modernize the rambling "ell" of a distinguished Connecticut farmhouse by providing within it a new kitchen and family dining area, two bedrooms, a family room, one-and-a-half baths, a laundry and workspace, and a two-car garage. In a later phase, the clients asked for a large "summer room."

As the eighth generation of the same family to occupy the house since it was built in 1746, the owners wanted exterior renovations and fenestration to be reasonably true to the dwelling's original period. They asked that interior renovations be sympathetic to Colonial architecture yet spacious, sunny, and up-to-date. They preferred passive solar heating, but not at the expense of colonial fenestration.

Because the "ell" was found to be an impractical configuration, the architects removed most of it. To take its place they designed a more compact and well-insulated "ell" with free-standing post-and-beam interior architecture. It uses traditional joinery from the Colonial period combined with a modern organization of spokes. The post-and-beam structure extends beyond the "ell" to form a "summer room" incorporating an existing free-standing chimney. A new interior chimney and fireplace, built of cobblestones formerly used in Boston's Haymarket Square, are the symbolic heart of the house and enclose a staircase to the second floor.

The post-and-beam structure is pulled back from the south side of the "ell" to allow for maximum penetration of light. A black slate floor on a concrete slab collects heat during the day and radiates it at night. In accordance with the owners' wishes, fenestration is kept within Colonial-style limits, recalling the windows of a barn or carriage house, and skylights admit large amounts of natural light.

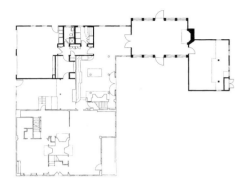

FIRST FLOOR PLAN

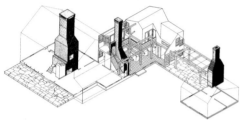

AXONOMETRIC

RIGHT: The fireplace was built with cobblestones from Boston's Haymarket Square. Colonial joinery techniques make a vertical and airy space.
Photo: Cervin Robinson

OPPOSITE, TOP: A stair winds its way behind the new fireplace and under a stone arch to a system of second-floor bridges.
Photo: Chad Floyd

OPPOSITE, BOTTOM: At the center of the kitchen is a seating area warmed by the fire.
Photo: Joseph Standart

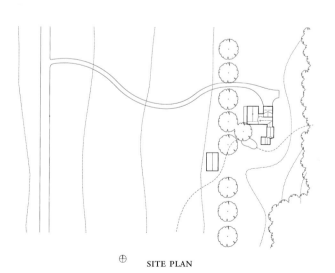

SITE PLAN

$\mathcal{B}$iomedical Research Laboratory

Neurogen Corporation
Branford, Connecticut

FIRST FLOOR PLAN

This new research laboratory was created within a 30-year-old industrial building. The structure was selected in part because it contained some office space, which could be used without renovation, and a high warehouse space, which could be renovated into two floors of laboratories. The owner was moving from an existing crowded building with low ceilings and virtually no windows or daylight and wanted the new facility to correct these conditions.

The challenge was to provide an interesting, naturally lighted work place with a feeling of openness in a nearly windowless warehouse filled with mechanical equipment. Among the design devices are a large central skylight over a two-story light well; office windows opening onto the central day-lit space; and the use of suspended ceilings only in laboratories and offices. In addition, the architects painted the entire underside of the roof and overhead mechanical equipment white, and used two colors of lighting: high-pressure sodium and metal halide. They directed the light sources—some warm, some cool—upward. The result is indirect illumination that gives the feeling of being outdoors.

Four plaster piers rising through layers of structure and mechanical systems emphasize the space's verticality. The smooth blue monoliths also reflect and diffuse sunlight from the skylight to the spaces below and act as a screen on which are cast patterned shadows that change from hour to hour and season to season.

OPPOSITE: Perforated steel railings surround the second floor light well.
Photo: Jeff Goldberg/Esto

RIGHT: Blue pylons reflect light from the skylight down into first-floor spaces.
Photo: Jeff Goldberg/Esto

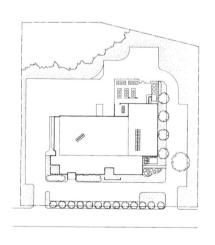

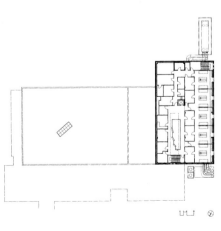

SITE PLAN   SECOND FLOOR PLAN

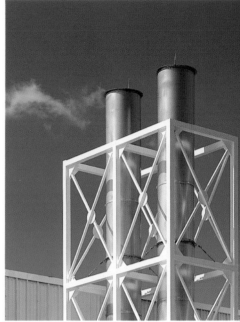

OPPOSITE, TOP: An air-exhaust unit and heat recovery system is located outside the building.
Photo: Jeff Goldberg/Esto

OPPOSITE, BOTTOM: The laboratories are compact but efficient.
Photo: Jeff Goldberg/Esto

ABOVE: The steel structural support of the air-exhaust stacks.
Photo: Jeff Goldberg/Esto

LEFT: Exposed mechanical systems, multi-colored offices, and a variety of different light sources make a formerly dark warehouse into a pleasant library.
Photo: Steve Rosenthal

$\mathcal{L}$ong View

This 12,500-square-foot house sits high on a mountain shelf overlooking a valley. A Gothic Revival mansion once occupied the extraordinary site and some of its great beech and maple trees remain.

Four rambling pavilions run north to south to take advantage of views of the cliff to the west and of a pond and mountaintop to the east. Long, steep roofs have dormers to reduce the apparent bulk as seen from the valley below. The two middle pavilions open toward the west to afford better views and to create an entry courtyard. Facing the driveway and the discrete doors of the north-facing garage, a tapered entry hall extends into the court in a gesture of greeting. The durable-looking house is clad in dark brown brick and has a green and purple slate roof, steel-framed windows, and French doors. Large overhanging eaves let in winter sun and provide shade in summer.

Home to a family of four, the house is zoned so that each precinct has its own colors and finishes. The main rooms are finished in a variety of natural woods. The family room and kitchen have cherry flooring with light maple cabinets, shelving, and ceiling boards. The formal rooms are darker, with cherry plank walls in the living room, African mahogany finishes in the study, and cherry trim elsewhere. Configured in a variety of shapes that collide in places to dramatize movement through the house, the public rooms offer surprising vistas.

The children's bedrooms and a guest bedroom are upstairs, while a parent's suite is located on the first floor at the north end of the house.

OPPOSITE: The large studio window faces north, overlooking the rest of the house across the entry court.

Photo: Jeff Goldberg/Esto

RIGHT: The entry hall tapers toward a stair, which has a built-in "bridal balcony" for greeting guests or throwing bouquets. The woodwork is cherry.

Photo: Jeff Goldberg/Esto

OPPOSITE: The entry drive curves up to a court where the front door is announced by a porte-cochere.
Photo: Jeff Goldberg/Esto

RIGHT: The garage and studio are the first part of the house seen from the driveway. They are simple in form and scaled like a cottage.
Photo: Jeff Goldberg/Esto

BELOW: Long View perches on the crest of a hill sloping down to a pond on the east. Slate shingle roofs with large eaves hide the dwelling's mass and block summer sun.
Photo: Jeff Goldberg/Esto

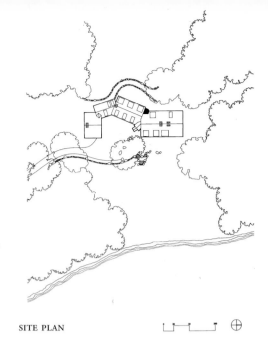

SITE PLAN

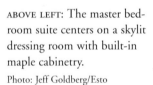

ABOVE LEFT: The master bedroom suite centers on a skylit dressing room with built-in maple cabinetry.

Photo: Jeff Goldberg/Esto

ABOVE RIGHT: The powder room is finished in mahogany and pink granite with brass fittings. Doorknobs throughout the house are rubbed bronze.

Photo: Jeff Goldberg/Esto

RIGHT: The living room is large, oval-paneled in cherry, and punched with openings. The fireplace, which appears to present itself at a random angle, offers a sitting stoop and wood storage.

Photo: Jeff Goldberg/Esto

ABOVE: The study is dark with mahogany paneling, bookcases, and desk. Gray granite surrounds the fireplace. The mantel gently curves out from the wall plane.

Photo: Jeff Goldberg/Esto

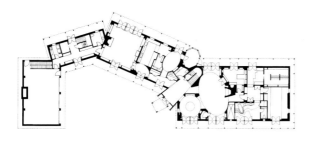

FIRST FLOOR PLAN

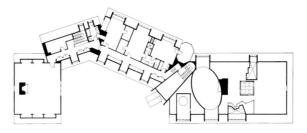

SECOND FLOOR PLAN

Discovery Research Center

DeKalb Plant Genetics Corporation
Stonington, Connecticut

ABOVE: The use of a variety of colors appears to break a large mass into smaller elements.
Photo: Jeff Goldberg/Esto

OPPOSITE: Each greenhouse compartment is self-contained and climate-controlled by computer.
Photo: Jeff Goldberg/Esto

The architects designed this new facility for scientists developing strains of corn that resist disease, insects, and drought. The 54,000-square-foot program includes a laboratory building, a headhouse, an equipment building, and 12,000 square feet of compartmentalized greenhouses. The site allows for experimental cornfields and two future phases of expansion that will triple the size of the facility over the next 10 years.

The buildings' forms and colors and their relation to the site recall traditional barns and farm buildings, befitting the facility's purpose. The structures are arranged with the greenhouses facing south, taking advantage of daylight. Sensors allow the computerized lights and vents to activate as light and temperature conditions change. The linear headhouse includes areas for soil preparation and climate-controlled growth chambers.

Laboratories are located on the east side of the building; offices with large windows are on the west. While the equipment rooms, bathrooms, and dark-rooms form the central spine of the building, a three-story, skylit library is the focus of both vertical and horizontal circulation. The research sequence begins in second-floor labs with the identification of specific genetic characteristics of plant cells. The work then proceeds to first-floor labs, where tiny plants are grown from single cells. It then moves to headhouse growth chambers for small plants and on to the greenhouse or fields.

The buildings surround a service courtyard, the shipping/receiving and recycling area for the entire complex. This courtyard, which contains garages for farm equipment, can be secured with large wooden rolling doors. At $116 per square foot, the Discovery Research Center is very economical, thanks to a careful organization of functional spaces, use of traditional building materials, and mechanical systems that save energy through extensive heat and cold recovery.

LEFT: The central, skylit library serves also as a vertical and horizontal passageway.
Photo: Jeff Goldberg/Esto

BELOW: The vinyl floor in the lab corridor has an abstract corn pattern.
Photo: Jeff Goldberg/Esto

OPPOSITE: The foliage of Japanese maples closely matches the color of the stucco.
Photo: Jeff Goldberg/Esto

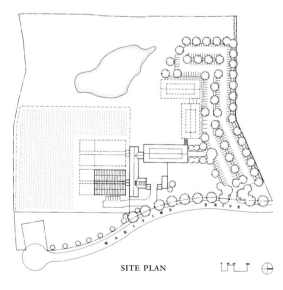

SITE PLAN

LEFT: The openings in the large rolling barn doors to the service yard align with the windows behind when the doors are fully open.

Photo: Jeff Goldberg/Esto

BELOW: The complex is designed to recall a cluster of agricultural buildings.

Photo: Jeff Goldberg/Esto

OPPOSITE: Landscaping consists simply of fields of experimental corn.

Photo: Jeff Goldberg/Esto

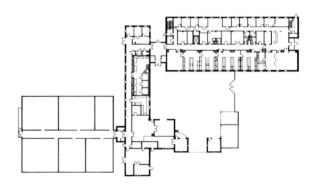

FIRST FLOOR PLAN

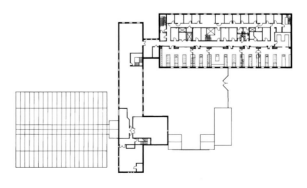

SECOND FLOOR PLAN

$\mathcal{A}$cademic Center and Honors Housing

TYPICAL FLOOR PLAN

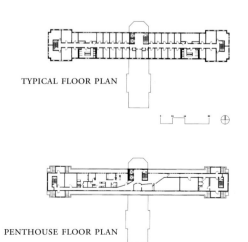

PENTHOUSE FLOOR PLAN

The program required a 400-bed dormitory for honor students, conducive to studying. The plan was to immediately construct the dormitory while master-planning the site for the addition of a 20,000-square-foot future academic building and a food-service facility.

The University of Toledo has a small number of fine Collegiate Gothic buildings, among them the University Hall Tower of 1931, which presides over a newer campus whose most memorable feature is the widespread use of buff-colored, native limestone.

As with many other college campuses, the post-war years—and especially the 1960s and '70s—brought to the University of Toledo rapid expansion, a tangle of architectural styles, and a resulting loss of coherence. Centerbrook's new dormitory, anticipated as a large and highly visible building, was seen as a way to begin to repair the fabric of the campus and resuscitate its architectural identity.

The six-story building stretches east to west just south of a small stream; enough space was left between it and the river to create an open lawn with trees.

The principal exterior material is a buff-colored brick that harmonizes with the university's older limestone buildings. The new structure's water table is rendered in a light-and-dark pattern of Flemish bond. The dormitory's steep roofs and Neo-Gothic proportions connect it with the older structures, but its liberal use of anodized aluminum makes it stand out. The roof is aluminum, as are all elements that earlier would have been cut stone, such as window frames and sills, the water table's deep cornice, and the building's tall chimneys. The sharply carved modern aluminum details change in the light and cast shadows in ways reminiscent of, but more abstract and snappy than, the high relief stone profiles of traditional Gothic buildings.

OPPOSITE: The dormitory recommences a dialogue between new campus buildings and the distinguished University Hall of 1931.

Photo: Jeff Goldberg/Esto

ABOVE: Supported by deep caissons atop a former landfill, the dormitory forms the southern edge of a large new campus green.

Photo: Jeff Goldberg/Esto

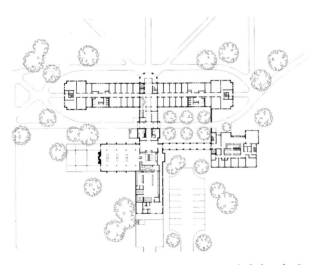

FIRST FLOOR PLAN

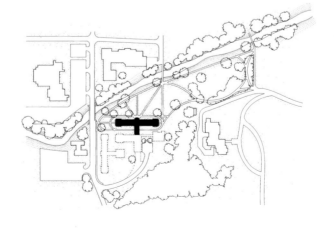

SITE PLAN

$\mathcal{E}$isenstein House

The owner of a farm in the central Midwest wanted a cottage deep in the hilly woods of his property overlooking a pond. He asked for three bedrooms, a study, kitchen, dining and living rooms, as well as a built-in garage. His budget was tight, but because he is a student of Medieval culture, he hoped for some references to the Middle Ages.

To keep costs at a minimum while providing the required spaces, Centerbrook configured the house as a simple square plan. The hip roof has generous eaves—in the tradition of the Prairie School—which provide abundant shading while allowing windows to remain open during summer storms. A central skylit rotunda brings light into the center of the house and distributes it through door openings and interior windows.

Brackets inside and out, gentle reminders of the owner's interest in the Middle Ages, give a sense of shelter to the entry roof and screen porch and make indoor passageways in a small house appear a little grander.

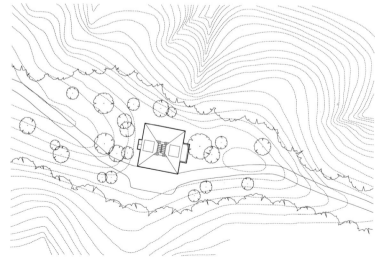

SITE PLAN   0 5 10 20

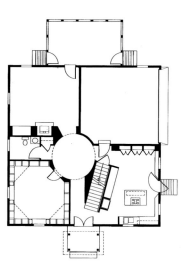

FIRST FLOOR PLAN

OPPOSITE, TOP: The Eisenstein House sits in a forest opening; every effort was made to preserve existing trees around the house. The driveway continues past the house as a lane and leads to ponds in the woods beyond.

Photo: Timothy Hursley

OPPOSITE, BOTTOM: The screen porch is situated under the master bedroom deck. Its three sides take advantage of prevailing summer breezes.

Photo: Timothy Hursley

LEFT, TOP: The large roof overhang shelters the house from the summer sun and allows windows to remain open in the rain. The efficient, blocky shape of the house is disguised by bracketing and the change from shingles to vertical cedar boards at mid-wall. The chimneys surrounding the central skylight are tapered to minimize their shadows.

Photo: Timothy Hursley

LEFT, BOTTOM: The round, skylit central hall brings light into the center of the house through doorways and interior windows. Simple stick bracketing and railings help mediate the eye's transition to the surrounding darker spaces.

Photo: Timothy Hursley

DNA Learning Center

ABOVE: The designers restored the exterior in keeping with local historic guidelines and added new lighting as well as an entry ramp.
Photo: Jeff Goldberg/Esto

OPPOSITE: The lecture hall accommodates science presentations, which use high-tech computer and video images, in a traditional and familiar setting.
Photo: Jeff Goldberg/Esto

The DNA Learning Center, which houses a national outreach program for the nearby Cold Spring Harbor Laboratory, was formerly an abandoned schoolhouse located in the center of the historic village of Cold Spring Harbor, New York. The center provides teachers and students an opportunity to study and experiment with the most recent developments in molecular biology.

Centerbrook renovated the 80-year-old Georgian Revival schoolhouse, restoring the outside to be in keeping with the historic guidelines of the village. The inside was remodeled to provide modern laboratories, exhibit space, and a lecture hall with state-of-the-art multimedia capabilities.

The interior character borrows from the characteristics of the original building and the surrounding village. Hints of the building's current use are suggested through symbols of genetic research: exterior ramp posts resemble bands of DNA, and interior torcherès are modeled after the double helix of DNA. The names of future Nobel Prize-winning biologists will be painted into the auditorium frieze.

As noted by the Learning Center's director, David A. Micklos, "Many science facilities are out of context with the architecture of their urban surroundings and appear unstuck in time, perhaps in a subtle way perpetuating the stereotype of science as an ivory tower out of touch with mainstream culture. We believe that this building sends the healthier message that science is forward-looking, yet rooted in time and culture."

OPPOSITE: The renovated lobby provides niches for visitors' coats and access to the exhibit space. The exhibit space has been painted, by staff and students, to resemble the inside of a cell.
Photo: Jeff Goldberg/Esto

RIGHT: The auditorium torcherès mimic the double-helix strands of DNA.
Photo: Jeff Goldberg/Esto

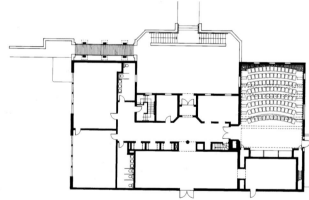

FIRST FLOOR PLAN

*T*he Amos Tuck School of Business Administration

Byrne Hall fits neatly into a neo-Georgian campus that has long been a source of pride to the Tuck School. But the new building does not duplicate the rest of the campus. Byrne Hall is closely integrated with the neighboring Stell Hall, a former dining hall converted to a spacious common room, and with Murdough, a classroom building. But although Centerbrook's new hall blends with neighboring buildings in appearance and is physically connected to two of them, it is still special in its own right. Built into a steep hill, its up-slope side completes the fourth wall of a small quadrangle, by means of a one-story facade featuring a centered entry vestibule flanked by a pair of low brick wings. An off-center octagonal dome peeks over the roof.

Byrne Hall is built of sturdy, water-struck brick laid up in three patterns of Flemish bond with contrasting red brick as counterpoint. Its roofs are slate, and its dormers are trimmed in white.

The building combines a 300-person dining hall with a variety of academic spaces, including two 75-person state-of-the-art auditorium classrooms, three 40-person classrooms, 12 seminar rooms, and several break-out lounge spaces.

OPPOSITE: The octagonal dining room has a Chinois
balustrade.
Photo: Jeff Goldberg/Esto

ABOVE: Two-story additions on
both sides of the neo-Georgian
Tuck Hall provide accessible
indoor connections while
improving the proportions of
the original.
Photo: Jeff Goldberg/Esto

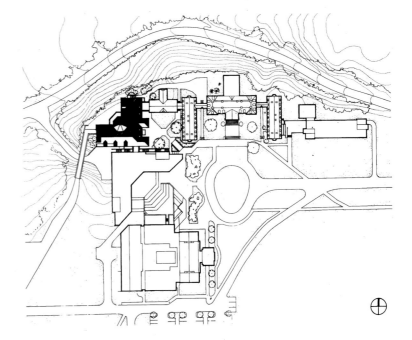

SITE PLAN

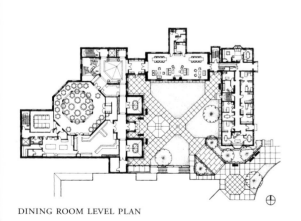

DINING ROOM LEVEL PLAN

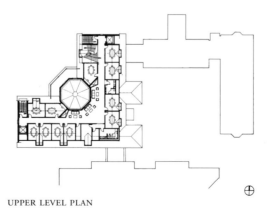

UPPER LEVEL PLAN

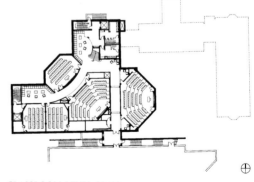

CLASSROOM LEVEL PLAN

OPPOSITE: Byrne Hall (left) is made to appear shorter than the historic Stell Hall (center) despite the five stories of its down-slope side.

Photo: Jeff Goldberg/Esto

RIGHT: The dining room's domed roof peeks out from behind Byrne Hall.

Photo: Jeff Goldberg/Esto

ABOVE: The new 40,000-square-foot Byrne Hall is tucked in snugly among several buildings to form the fourth side of a shady quadrangle. Only one-quarter of the building's height is visible from this view.
Photo: Jeff Goldberg/Esto

RIGHT: Boomerang-shaped ceiling elements in this 75-person classroom provide up- and down-lighting to fit many teaching situations.
Photo: Jeff Goldberg/Esto

OPPOSITE: The work included restoring the interior of Stell Hall, formerly the dining room of the Tuck School. Byrne Hall's grand stair is visible on-axis in the distance.
Photo: Jeff Goldberg/Esto

EAST WEST SECTION PLAN

RIGHT: The grand stair in Byrne Hall twists its way with verve through four stories.
Photo: Jeff Goldberg/Esto

OPPOSITE: The octagonal dining room has a large chandelier disguising energy-saving fluorescent bulbs behind lampshades.
Photo: Jeff Goldberg/Esto

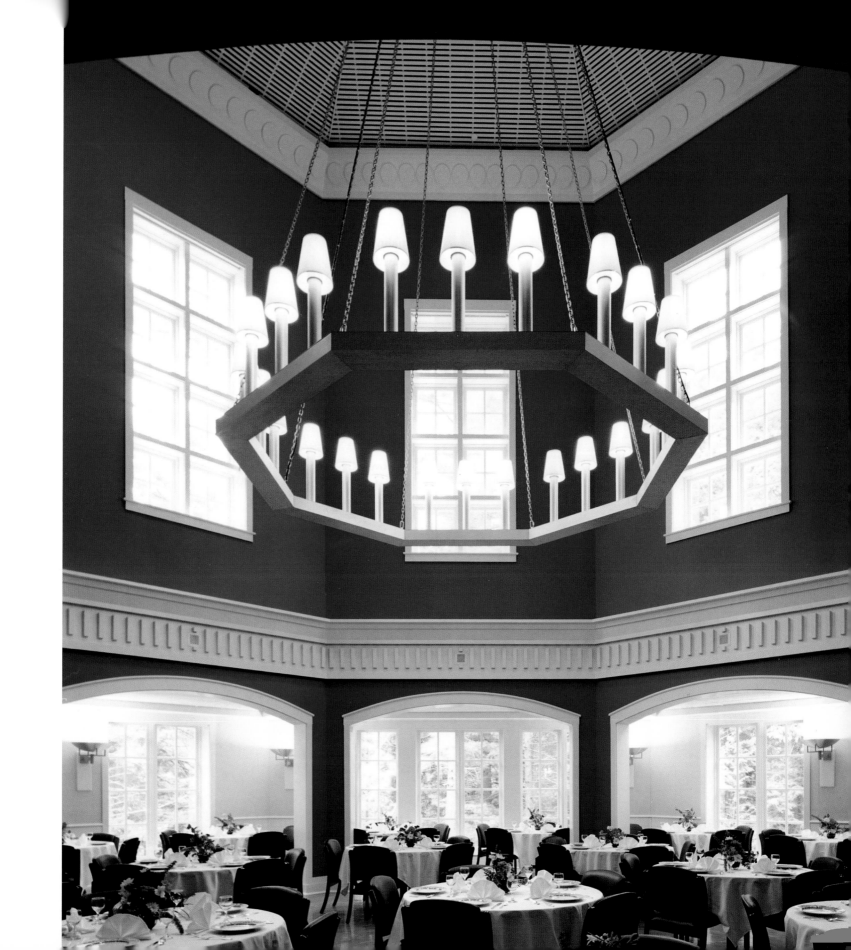

RIGHT: The character of the building changes at dusk.
Photo: Jeff Goldberg/Esto

OPPOSITE, TOP: The senior scientist's office has a beautiful view of Cold Spring Harbor.
Photo: Jeff Goldberg/Esto

OPPOSITE, BOTTOM: From a distance, the roof appears suspended above the historic building.
Photo: Jeff Goldberg/Esto

FIRST FLOOR PLAN

SECOND FLOOR PLAN

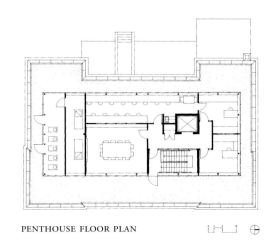

PENTHOUSE FLOOR PLAN

Ridgway House

Most of this residence is built on the foundation of an earlier house. It is situated between a busy street and a small pond, and using an old foundation allowed the house to be built farther from the street and closer to the pond than would otherwise have been possible.

Major living spaces are oriented away from the street and facing the pond. On the first floor, the living and dining areas, the family room, the kitchen, and the master bedroom all overlook the pond; on the second floor, all bedrooms face the pond. Facing the street are only a small study and one end of the living room on the first floor; dressing rooms and bathrooms are on the second. The character of the house changes from front to back: windows facing the street are few and very large. These, together with the stylized Greek Revival trim and detailing, make the street facade appear smaller than it is and formal, even stand-offish, to the neighbors. In the back of the house many windows face the pond in a more open, friendly, bring-the-outdoors-in manner.

Within, a screen of columns helps to articulate the living room, and columns and a shallow dome define the dining room. The placement of columns, however, permits the dining table to be considerably enlarged, accommodating many guests without sacrificing the character of the room. The kitchen and family room are, appropriately, more informal and less classical.

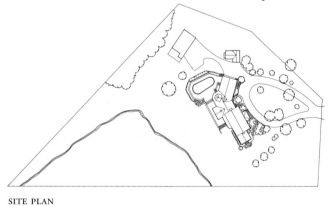

SITE PLAN

OPPOSITE: Overscaled openings and trim help the house to appear smaller than it really is from the street.
Photo: Jeff Goldberg/Esto

ABOVE: A domed ceiling establishes a formal space for dining in an otherwise open and informal plan.
Photo: Jeff Goldberg/Esto

LEFT: The rooms across the west side of the house overlook the pond and marshes.
Photo: Jeff Goldberg/Esto

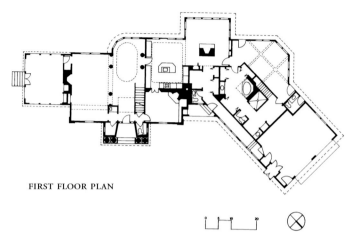

FIRST FLOOR PLAN

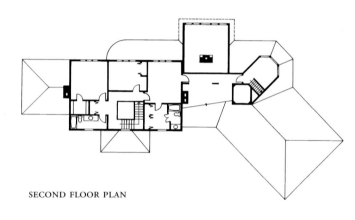

SECOND FLOOR PLAN

OPPOSITE: The kitchen and family room look toward the pond through tall windows.
Photo: Jeff Goldberg/Esto

LEFT, TOP: Screens made of columns articulate living spaces without restricting furniture placement or human activity.
Photo: Jeff Goldberg/Esto

LEFT, BOTTOM: The columned porch anchors one end of a vista through the house toward the pond.
Photo: Jeff Goldberg/Esto

*K*washa Lipton Offices

These interior renovations expanded the headquarters of a corporate-benefits consulting firm that serves many Fortune 500 companies. Located on the Fort Lee Palisades in New Jersey, the firm enjoys extraordinary views of the George Washington Bridge, the Hudson River, and Manhattan.

Initially, 20,000 square feet of new offices were added on the building's fourth floor with a new 10-station computer lab, a training room, conference rooms, and a lunch room. The budget was modest, requiring substantial re-use of the previous tenant's room arrangements. Later additions include a first-floor phone-answering center with acoustic "clouds," multimedia rooms, and new offices on other floors.

The new reception area adjoins the elevator lobby, which has splayed walls to highlight the axial view of the bridge outside. Three Josef Hoffmann chairs form a small seating area opening to the computer lab and conference rooms, the most frequent visitor destinations. Historic construction photographs of the George Washington Bridge line the walls.

Workstations are aligned throughout the building's length to allow team flexibility. On the fourth floor, to make identifiable "neighborhoods" and celebrate Fort Lee (which was the home of the Palisades Amusement Park), glass dividers in the shapes of roller coasters flank each eight-station grouping.

In response to requests made by staff members during workshops, muted but rich colors were used throughout. Dark green carpets play off copper blinds, soft green file cabinets, and other furniture. Rectangular grids and dots, signature motifs for the company, are repeated on doors, ceilings, and wall screens. Conference tables, designed by the architect, recall the bridge outside. Overall, the offices are businesslike but cheerful.

OPPOSITE, TOP: The phone center at Kwasha Lipton has acoustic "clouds" and ceiling panels to absorb noise from an adjacent highway. Desks are arranged in bands that weave through the existing irregular floor plan.
Photo: Jeff Goldberg/Esto

OPPOSITE, BOTTOM: Glass block walls add the sparkle of daylight to the interior reception area.
Photo: Jeff Goldberg/Esto

LEFT: The entrance to one of the new office floors has neon tubes twisting behind glass block walls to cheer users.
Photo: Jeff Goldberg/Esto

BELOW: A waiting area is lined with historic photos of the construction of the George Washington Bridge, which looms outside the building.
Photo: Jeff Goldberg/Esto

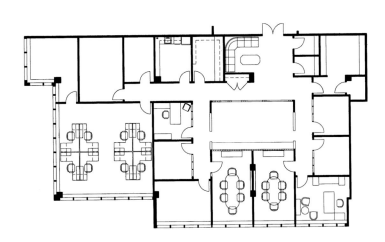

BECKER ROONEY OFFICES PLAN

ABOVE: A gridded window
shows off the computer test
bank while shielding a tangle
of wires below.
Photo: Jeff Goldberg/Esto

OPPOSITE, TOP: Another conference room has a curving wall of
windows to allow prospective
clients to watch and discuss
office activity. The windows
can be covered for privacy.
Photo: Jeff Goldberg/Esto

OPPOSITE, BOTTOM: A confer-
ence room overlooking the
George Washington Bridge has
a table inspired by bridge con-
struction that was designed by
Mark Simon for Gilbert
Furniture.
Photo: Jeff Goldberg/Esto

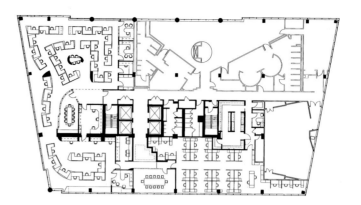

FIRST FLOOR PLAN

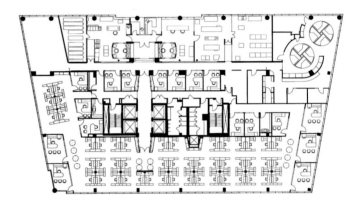

SECOND FLOOR PLAN

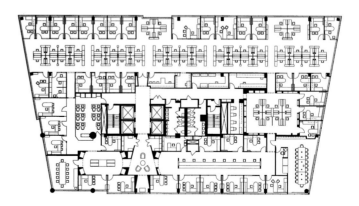

FOURTH FLOOR PLAN

$\mathcal{L}$ender School of Business Center

Quinnipiac College
Hamden, Connecticut

ABOVE: The hallway of the mass communication wing passes by the radio and television studios providing passersby the pleasures of a window shopper.

Photo: Jeff Goldberg/Esto

OPPOSITE: Student lounges, team study rooms, and classrooms are clearly arranged along a distinctive path, where multiple television monitors broadcast international news and business reports.

Photo: Jeff Goldberg/Esto

This low-lying building creates the northern boundary of the college's main quadrangle and is divided into two wings, separated by an arched portal that provides a ceremonial gateway into the quadrangle from the college's main entrance to the north. The east wing houses the Business School classrooms, an executive seminar room, and the student resource room, while the west wing comprises the Ed McMahon Mass Communications Center and faculty offices. An outdoor globe, built of steel and glass and supported on brick columns, is integral to the gateway and marks the entrance to the two wings of the center. It is also a symbol of the international direction that the study of business is taking at the college. The building has been kept to one story to maintain the powerful visual presence of the landmark Sleeping Giant Mountain.

The building's various functions clearly are arranged along a distinctive path that extends from under the globe into both wings of the building. In the classroom wing, several lounges on the edge of the circulation spine encourage spontaneous gatherings and conversation among students and faculty. Outside each classroom is a bench and small blackboard where students and teachers can meet after class to discuss lingering questions. Small team study rooms are located along the curving portion of the path and share daylight from clerestory windows that bring sunshine into the core of the building. Three case-method lecture halls, with seating in the round, take the focus away from the teacher and encourage interaction among students in simulation of real-life business dealings.

In the mass communications wing the hallway, again edged with small lounges, is a serpentine frieze adorned with vintage microphones. The hallway passes the windowed radio studio and terminates at a circular lounge that allows visitors and students to view the master control room and television studios beyond.

THIS PAGE, CLOCKWISE FROM TOP: A clerestory ribbon-window brings daylight into the building's core. Benches and blackboards outside each classroom provide a place for discussions after class.
Photo: Jeff Goldberg/Esto

Three case-method lecture halls are carefully configured to facilitate interaction between members of the class to simulate real-life business dealings.
Photo: Jeff Goldberg/Esto

Six team study rooms are arranged along the hallway. Like small porches on a street, they are sociable places to be.
Photo: Jeff Goldberg/Esto

ABOVE: The low building
spreads its wings, enclosing the
northern boundary of the main
quadrangle and allowing the
Sleeping Giant Mountain to
maintain its vigilant gaze upon
the campus.

Photo: Jeff Goldberg/Esto

RIGHT: A pavilion collects visitors arriving from the parking lot and provides them with a map of the campus.
Photo: Jeff Goldberg/Esto

OPPOSITE: The globe also serves as symbol of the center's international mission.
Photo: Jeff Goldberg/Esto

BELOW: The center completes the enclosure of the main quadrangle by aligning its east facade with that of the library. A suntrap offers its south-facing walls to loungers on cool days.
Photo: Jeff Goldberg/Esto

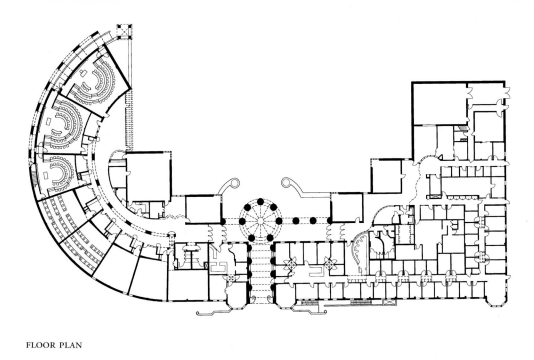

FLOOR PLAN

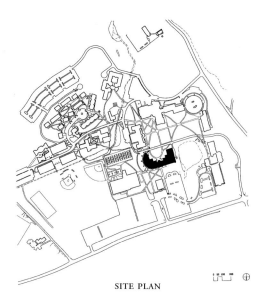

SITE PLAN

LEFT: The rotunda's landmark globe marks the main entry into the campus from the north.

Photo: Jeff Goldberg/Esto

OPPOSITE: The globe is a beacon, while four clerestory monitors bring indirect daylight into seminar rooms.

Photo: Jeff Goldberg/Esto

RIGHT: The bottom half of the bathroom window provides privacy, the top furnishes views and ventilation. Wood and glass wall sconces resemble Japanese lanterns.
Photo: Jeff Goldberg/Esto

BELOW: Exposed cedar framing, expressive of the owner's Japanese heritage, defines the sitting area and provides an armature for uplighting the fabric panels.
Photo: Jeff Goldberg/Esto

EXISTING FLOOR PLAN

FIRST FLOOR PLAN

ABOVE: The great room opens the house to the landscape. Fabric panels, diffusing light and sound, have curves similar to those of a violin.

Photo: Jeff Goldberg/Esto

OPPOSITE: Nauticus' lighting, cool on its exterior and warmer at covered exterior spaces, gives it the appearance of a giant sea serpent rising from the water at night.
Photo: Jeff Goldberg/Esto

RIGHT: The north side of the building suggests a futuristic aircraft carrier at dock.
Photo: Jeff Goldberg/Esto

BELOW: The large Theme Theater has a movable screen that rolls into a hidden wall pocket at film's end, uncovering a huge window facing the harbor.
Photo: Jeff Goldberg/Esto

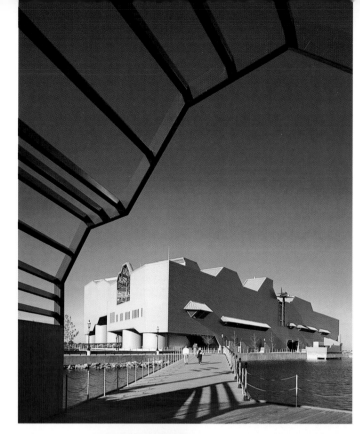

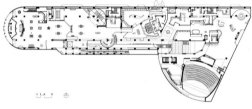

THIRD FLOOR PLAN

ABOVE LEFT: Practically the entire pier's perimeter can be used to dock exhibit vessels of all kinds, from a 600-foot naval cruiser, to "Tall Ships," to research boats and small pleasure craft.
Photo: Jeff Goldberg/Esto

ABOVE RIGHT: Entry to the museum is from 70-foot-long wooden gangplanks over reflecting pools that spill toward the river. The building arches high overhead to let light come deep inside.
Photo: Jeff Goldberg/Esto

LEFT: The Wonderhall balcony soffits are corrugated metal, with ribbing similar to the exterior cladding. Patterns in the terrazzo floor suggest ships or water life.
Photo: Jeff Goldberg/Esto

OPPOSITE: At the "prow" of the building, an exterior deck has mounted telescopes that make the river yet another exhibit. Historic storm warning lights, salvaged from one of Norfolk's older buildings, serve as a "hood ornament" while alerting ships to storms.
Photo: Jeff Goldberg/Esto

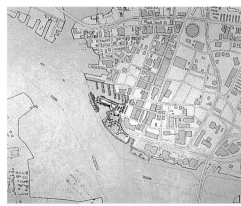

SITE PLAN

ABOVE: Railings are bent into wave forms and tilt inward to prevent children from leaning over. The mahogany is reminiscent of ships' rails.
Photo: Jeff Goldberg/Esto

RIGHT: The third-floor exhibit hall stretches out toward the river to cover the Celebration Pavilion, which offers close-up views of shipping activity protected from rain and heat.
Photo: Jeff Goldberg/Esto

RIGHT: The central atrium space, the "Wonderhall," introduces the various elements of the museum. It is capped by a giant skylight and filled with a Piranesian assortment of people mover, stairs, and balconies.

Photo: Jeff Goldberg/Esto

ABOVE: On its entry side, the
building sits on five fat piers, as
would a deep-sea oil rig. It has
been designed to fit in with the
industrial character of the
working harbor as well as with
the more refined parks and
downtown buildings nearby.

Photo: Jeff Goldberg/Esto

OPPOSITE: The people mover
slopes gently over two stories
through a series of bulkhead
arches to the third floor exhibit
space. The arches have subtly
changing colors and are occa-
sionally interrupted by windows
with views of the harbor.

Photo: Jeff Goldberg/Esto

$\mathcal{W}$atson House

The clients are Dr. and Mrs. James D. Watson: she is a writer, he is the co-discoverer of the structure of deoxyribonucleic acid (DNA) and the president of the Cold Spring Harbor laboratory. Their new house stands on the laboratory's grounds overlooking the Long Island Sound in an old neighborhood of large estates.

The Watsons requested that the house have a strong presence in the landscape and also a dramatic entrance on the west side; shaded porches on the north and south sides; a separate two-car garage connected underground to the house; a light-filled stairway; a library for him; a study for her; a flexible flow of first-floor spaces for entertaining, plus large dining and living rooms; and ample display space for art and memorabilia.

Centerbrook took its design cues from the clients' preference for elegant yet comfortable English Regency houses, symmetry, the unexpected spatial interplay achieved by architect Sir John Soane, high ceilings, tall double-hung windows, and display niches and shelves. The yellow-orange color of the exterior stucco was chosen for its warmth.

A wide porch wraps the kitchen, allowing Dr. Watson's study to overlook the landscaped grounds, which were originally designed by landscape architect Frederick Law Olmsted and partially restored by Centerbrook and landscape architect Morgan Wheelock. The living room and master bedroom have views of Long Island Sound.

The interior's most striking features are four corner skylights atop the central stair that, resting above mirrored corners, reflect patches of sunlight into the stair hall. On the second floor, the skylights, combined with high interior windows surrounding the second-floor central hall, supply bedrooms with an added source of natural illumination.

OPPOSITE: Garage and house
frame a view of the harbor
from the driveway.
Photo: Jeff Goldberg/Esto

ABOVE: Generous overhangs and
porches control the summer
sun.
Photo: Jeff Goldberg/Esto

LEFT: The high ceiling of the master bedroom receives light from the central hall.
Photo: Jeff Goldberg/Esto

BELOW: A perfect vantage point above the harbor.
Photo: Jeff Goldberg/Esto

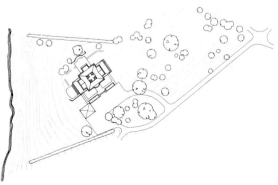

SITE PLAN

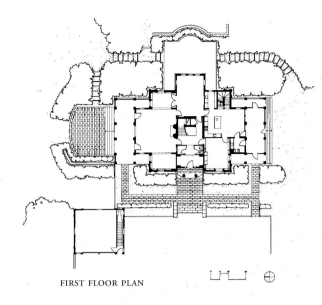

FIRST FLOOR PLAN

ABOVE: The central hallway illuminates the second floor library.
Photo: Jeff Goldberg/Esto

RIGHT: An eclectic mix of antique chairs surround the dining table.
Photo: Jeff Goldberg/Esto

ABOVE: Symmetry is an
important attribute in both
architecture and biology.
Photo: Jeff Goldberg/Esto

OPPOSITE: Tapered ribs give
square wooden columns
texture.
Photo: Jeff Goldberg/Esto

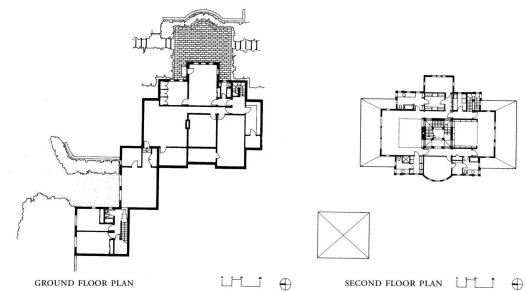

GROUND FLOOR PLAN   SECOND FLOOR PLAN

$\mathcal{P}$fizer, Incorporated

ABOVE: The entry court's gateway is the prime entry point for automobiles and pedestrians.
Photo: Jeff Goldberg/Esto

OPPOSITE: A white steel superstructure in the shape of a large oval creates an unmistakable point of arrival to visitors.
Photo: Jeff Goldberg/Esto

Pfizer's large industrial plant in Groton, Connecticut was converted in 1946 from wartime service as a submarine yard to chemical and pharmaceutical production. By 1991 its main gate had become a bottleneck of tank trucks, automobiles, railroad tank cars, and foot traffic. A new entrance was needed to present a positive and memorable image, relieve congestion, and provide efficient administrative offices.

To limit main gate traffic, reduce conflicting uses, and enlarge the site, the architects relocated the existing truck scale and employee entry, and rerouted a railroad spur. They converted a concrete frame warehouse into administrative offices, giving vendors access without compromising security. The designers clad the exterior in a wall of windows without mullions, conveying the appearance of a silver cube. In its lobby, visitor functions are marked by non-orthogonal, box-like vestibules, which are beige-colored, while the company's official blue color is used to demarcate the orthogonal column grid.

Adjacent to the administration building is a new oval automobile court, enclosed by a steel superstructure reminiscent of the plant's maritime past. To promote legibility, the enclosure is painted white, as are all curved elements in the plant, such as pipes and tanks; beige and silver are reserved for rectilinear elements. Small, vertical fins in the structure's infill panels allow security officers to see the street while blocking views into the plant.

ABOVE LEFT: The lobby is dominated by a free-form stair interwoven among columns in Pfizer's blue company color.
Photo: Jeff Goldberg/Esto

ABOVE RIGHT: Beige, box-like elements protruding into the lobby house the reception desk and foyers for the lecture hall, conference room, and plant access door.
Photo: Jeff Goldberg/Esto

LEFT: The lobby stair cascades around one of the blue columns.
Photo: Jeff Goldberg/Esto

OPPOSITE: A steel entry canopy penetrates the oval for admission of visitors into the administation building.
Photo: Jeff Goldberg/Esto

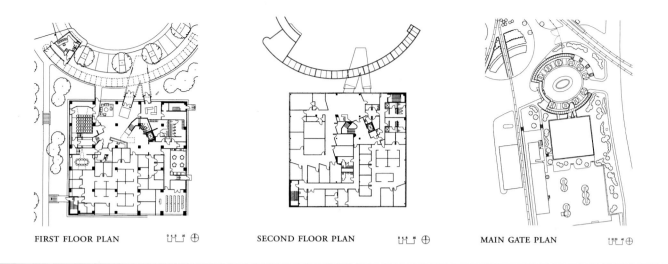

FIRST FLOOR PLAN

SECOND FLOOR PLAN

MAIN GATE PLAN

LEFT: This new 80,000-square-foot technology building at the center of the plant is nestled among white-painted tanks and pipe racks.
Photo: Jeff Goldberg/Esto

BELOW: One of several new computer control rooms for automated production.
Photo: Jeff Goldberg/Esto

OPPOSITE: This small building is the entrance point for most plant employees.
Photo: Jeff Goldberg/Esto

*G*ordon House

ABOVE: The Gordon House resides in an island landscape of wild roses and bull briars. The rear faces the sea across a marsh and pond; hip roofs merge the house with low-lying scrub and shelter it from furious winds.

Photo: Langdon Clay

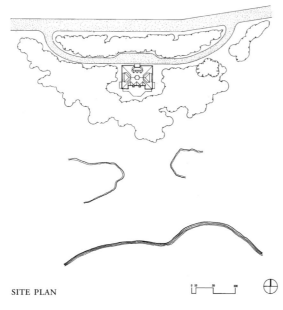

SITE PLAN

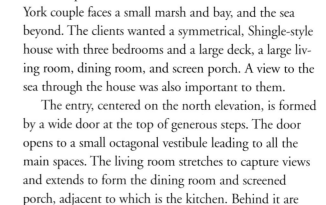

The 3,100-square-foot summer vacation house for a New York couple faces a small marsh and bay, and the sea beyond. The clients wanted a symmetrical, Shingle-style house with three bedrooms and a large deck, a large living room, dining room, and screen porch. A view to the sea through the house was also important to them.

The entry, centered on the north elevation, is formed by a wide door at the top of generous steps. The door opens to a small octagonal vestibule leading to all the main spaces. The living room stretches to capture views and extends to form the dining room and screened porch, adjacent to which is the kitchen. Behind it are stairs to the master bedroom deck.

The first floor opens to a wide deck, part of which is covered by the roof overhangs. The deck is edged with a continuous seat, beneath which large boulders from the site have been stacked as riprap protection for the dwelling's substructure and basement.

Upstairs, the master bedroom offers water views from large dormers as well as from its deck. The master bedroom has a comfortable walk-in dressing room and bath. The large guest bedroom and smaller study are graced with complex ceiling configurations formed by the intersections of the hip roof and dormers.

Because they created substantial protective overhangs, the architects were able to design a very glassy house that can admit cooling southwest breezes, despite the site's fierce winds and rain. Windows in walls and bays are staggered from the first floor to the second, giving the house a syncopated rhythm.

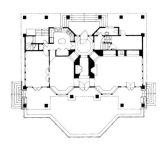

FIRST FLOOR PLAN

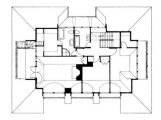

SECOND FLOOR PLAN

ABOVE LEFT: The over-scaled dormers offer the bedrooms wide views. The dormer arches cut into the hipped roof as in a cottage.

Photo: Langdon Clay

ABOVE RIGHT: The living room has a granite fireplace and a bay window with a seat overlooking the sea.

Photo: Langdon Clay

LEFT: The drive comes right up to the wide front steps, which lead to a front door with views through the house to the sea. Here dormers are smaller and ganged together in marked contrast to the rear of the house.

Photo: Langdon Clay

The Carl and Ruth Shapiro Admissions Center

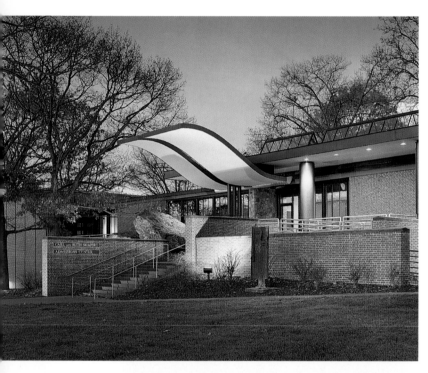

The 10,000-square-foot Shapiro Admissions Center was originally designed in the 1950s by Harrison and Abramovitz as Mailman Hall, a plain-looking commuter student retreat. To renovate it for admissions, the university felt the building needed to be more visible, easy to identify, accessible to all, and inviting. Centerbrook transformed the 1950s building into a lively new visitors' center rendered in a fresh International Style. The new design contains the admissions department, including a large reception room, a presentation hall, conference rooms, fourteen interview offices, and a processing/clerical center.

Across the front of the building, a flat canopy shades the south-facing windows and gives shelter to the stairs and ramp. To mark the entry from a distance and to cover the lower portion of the stairs, a second curved and more dramatic canopy springs out from below the first. An exterior skylight illuminates the front door, and the word "Admissions" in stainless steel tubing appears above the flat canopy roof.

Inside, a reception desk is fashioned from the intersecting planes of walls and floating storage cabinets, a bow to the Bauhaus. On the reception room walls, cherry paneling was restored and extended. The furnishings are a mix of comfortable leather couches and tables custom-designed by the architect.

Interview offices are simple but elegant. Where possible, the original exterior brick walls are exposed.

The processing center, a light-filled, open workspace with twelve desks, was created from a collection of dark basement rooms by adding bands of large north- and south-facing windows.

In most of the rooms lighting is inexpensive but spirited. Standard black-boxed fluorescent fixtures hang from the ceilings to cross above and below each other at right angles, another modernist enthusiasm.

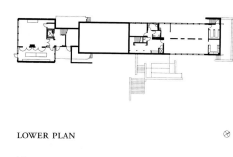

LOWER PLAN

ENTRY PLAN

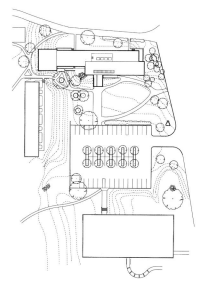

SITE PLAN

OPPOSITE, TOP: The accessible front door ramps weave in and out of orthogonal brick walls, blending them with the entry steps.

Photo: Steve Rosenthal

OPPOSITE, BOTTOM: The architects designed the furniture for the Admissions Center. The conference room has a mahogany-topped table and sideboard and a sculptural coat rack. The lights are inexpensive fluorescent "boxes" arranged in a playful three dimensional pattern.

Photo: Steve Rosenthal

ABOVE: The reception desk in the waiting room, like a de Stijl construction, has intersecting colored planes that are echoed by the lighting, an abstract pattern of recessed fluorescents that dramatizes the ceiling.

Photo: Steve Rosenthal

LEFT: The new admissions center was designed to be easy to identify day and night. Stainless letters on the roof are bright and enliven the building. The entry canopy is uplit to mark the front door.

Photo: Steve Rosenthal

*H*ouse in the Hudson Valley

This large addition to a weekend retreat in the gently rolling hills of upstate New York extends outward from a nineteenth-century farmhouse that appears from the road as a string of traditional, connected barns. To passers-by on the road, the "barns" conceal the dwelling's large size and complexity. It contains a gymnasium and exercise rooms, a spa, a great room, a bunk room, an office, a summer room, gardens, terraces, a pool house, and a pool. The complex was designed to transport the owners out of their work-a-day city world to one of maximum physical and emotional comfort.

An informal entry gate leads into an intimate herb garden, where views of the whole complex unfold. Stone walls create outdoor terraces and places to sit overlooking the pool and pond. Inside, fir paneling and stylized "trees" used in the great room recall the owners' love affair with Adirondack lodges and the forests that surround their property. The bunk room perches in the upper reaches of the great room as might a tree house. Triple-hung windows convert the summer room into a screen porch on pleasant days. The gymnasium contains a half court for basketball and a windowed exercise room overlooking the vegetable garden, while the spa's Jacuzzi tub has a private view of the miniature Zen rock garden. The office, which has its own outdoor entrance, commands panoramic views of the property.

ABOVE: The original farmhouse hides the extensive additions, in deference to its rural neighborhood.
Photo: Brian Vanden Brink

LEFT: Triple-hung windows open up the walls of the new summer room to the hilltop breezes and aroma of the herb garden.
Photo: Brian Vanden Brink

OPPOSITE: The three buildings—appearing as connected barns when viewed from the road—command the hilltop overlook. The additions are joined to the original farmhouse by the enclosed herb garden and summer room.
Photo: Brian Vanden Brink

FIRST FLOOR PLAN

SITE PLAN

ABOVE: A covered connector to the additions provides an intimate "back door" entry as well as an enclosure protecting the herb garden from deer.
Photo: Brian Vanden Brink

ABOVE RIGHT: The kitchen in the existing farmhouse was redone with Shaker-style cabinets and granite countertops in fruit shapes.
Photo: Brian Vanden Brink

RIGHT: A second floor bunk room is poised in the "tree branches" of the great room.
Photo: Brian Vanden Brink

OPPOSITE: Douglas-fir paneling and "trees" in the great room recall mountain lodges and mysterious forests and provide a welcome retreat from city life.
Photo: Brian Vanden Brink

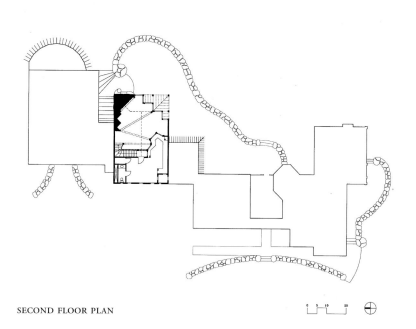

SECOND FLOOR PLAN

OPPOSITE: The stone fireplace in the great room is outfitted with a custom-designed screen and utensils that echo the room's motifs. Andirons were made with mica maple leaves that glow in the light of the fire.

Photo: Brian Vanden Brink

ABOVE RIGHT: The festive character of the great room is brought to light at night. The latticed roof overhang shades the tall corner windows during summer days.

Photo: Brian Vanden Brink

LEFT: Benches in the bunk room double as beds when the crowd gets large.

Photo: Brian Vanden Brink

ℛathskeller

This addition to the college's student center, known as the "Rathskeller," is located within the residential district of the campus. The addition takes on the status of a neighborhood pub. Large windows open onto a busy pedestrian street that links the residence halls and collects students headed toward the academic quadrangle. Wide plaza steps provide places to sit at the edge of the street.

The existing structure houses a renovated bar and new food emporium. The addition steps down the hill toward the street, creating several levels of varying size. In the "pavilion," used regularly for dancing, a deejay balcony perches above the entry doors. Large bronze lanterns, traditional in appearance, house a full array of nightclub lighting effects, including spotlights trained on the whirring blades of four ceiling fans, each mirrored to reflect sparkling light onto the ceiling.

ABOVE: The pub-like pavilion is a landmark on the street.
Photo: Robert Benson

OPPOSITE: The pavilion connects to an existing brick building and provides numerous places outdoors to sit and gather.
Photo: Robert Benson

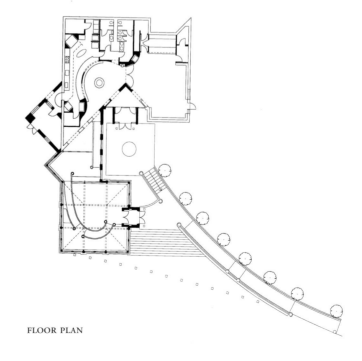

FLOOR PLAN

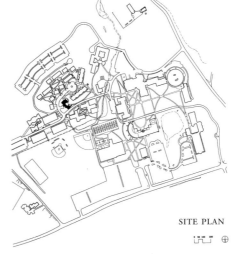

SITE PLAN

$\mathcal{P}$all Corporation Technical Center

The Fortune 500 client had purchased this once-abandoned warehouse with the idea of simply expanding its storage and laboratory space. Centerbrook persuaded the company to turn the building into the company's technical center.

Pall charged the architects with creating, on a limited budget, functional and attractive spaces for research laboratories and a training center, using materials suggestive of its cutting-edge products.

Modifications to the exterior were minimal. The architects focused on creating an entrance featuring a prominent overhang made of aluminum. On the second floor, the architects added windows and skylights to admit daylight. They also changed the exterior color from white to dark blue "to prevent the building from appearing top-heavy," says partner-in-charge Bill Grover. In addition, Centerbrook made extensive structural modifications and installed a centralized mechanical system that won rebates from local utilities for its energy-conscious design.

The interior configuration was driven by the need to separate spaces accessible to customers from those that are not. The principal circulation corridor, which runs from the main lobby to the rear of the building, serves all the public spaces and acts as a buffer between two rows of laboratories. At the corridor's midpoint is a skylit lobby, which is graced by a decorative stair and serves as the primary link between the ground floor and the second-floor training center. The second floor also contains offices and a television studio.

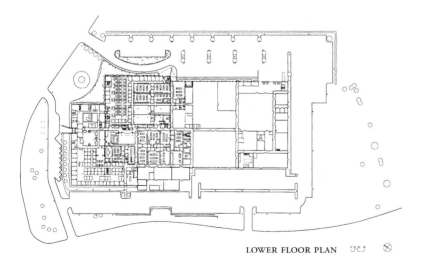

LOWER FLOOR PLAN

ABOVE LEFT: Stainless steel, used in many of the Pall products, is used here as a decorative material.

Photo: Robert Benson

ABOVE RIGHT: The presentation room displays filters as if they were jewelry.

Photo: Robert Benson

LEFT: The cantilevered blade of the main entry canopy speaks of Pall's "cutting edge" technology.

Photo: Robert Benson

OPPOSITE: Rooftop air exhaust-fan structure with stainless steel stacks.

Photo: Robert Benson

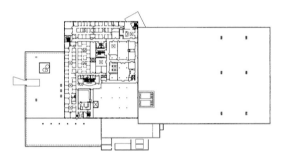

UPPER FLOOR PLAN

OPPOSITE, CLOCKWISE FROM TOP LEFT: Clear skylights allow executive diners to see the sky.
Photo: Robert Benson

A glass-walled central courtyard garden brings natural light into a conference room.
Photo: Robert Benson

Conference rooms deep in the center of the building get natural light.
Photo: Robert Benson

LEFT: A centrally located, two-story skylit lobby serves as the hub for horizontal and vertical circulation.
Photo: Robert Benson

BELOW: Perforated stainless steel symbolizes the filters that Pall manufactures.
Photo: Robert Benson

$\mathcal{P}$all Corporation Headquarters

OPPOSITE: Perforated metal panels are angled to diffuse and reflect west sunlight.

Photo: Jeff Goldberg/Esto

The world headquarters of this Fortune 500 manufacturer of specialized filters is located in a former Helena Rubenstein cosmetics factory from the 1950s. The corporation has more or less continuously modified its home office building as it has devised new products. The East Hills building contains not only corporate offices, but some sales and marketing staff. And it is here that Pall develops new products and the machinery for their manufacture before moving production to factories around the world.

Planning studies by Centerbrook and Pall Corporation resulted in the relocation of Pall's technical center to a renovated building in Port Washington, New York, and the redesign of the East Hills building. Pall needed a very flexible layout to handle reorganizations and reconfigurations upon short notice, and the building had an unnecessarily complicated mixture of mechanical, electrical, and plumbing systems as well as an inefficient floor plan with many windowless interior offices. The architects' changes included a new mechanical system and a huge water-deionizing system. They also added two new stair-towers so that second- and third-floor warehouse space could be converted into office space. The new offices are mostly open plan, with windows facing east and west.

The exterior skin of the new addition is brick with translucent panels that help to illuminate the manufacturing spaces within. Interior details such as stair railings and lighting fixtures were fabricated from stainless steel and perforated metal, symbolic of the filters made by Pall.

Residence Hall

The new residence hall for 486 students addressed two major concerns. The first, cost, was solved by creating rooms that each house four students and are economically arranged along double-loaded corridors on three floors. The furnishings in each small room were custom-designed to permit several possible arrangements, each one offering a division of the room into four private realms. Additionally, six large study lounges and eighteen small alcoves and window nooks provide a variety of getaways dispersed throughout the complex.

The second concern, the building's massive size, was resolved by creating three separate "houses," each with its own entry, each appearing small and house-like. The spaces between these houses create courtyards and suntraps, which break up the massiveness of the building. Each of the three houses has a distinctive interior, a major social space, and an identity matching its name: the Lodge, the Castle, and the Villa.

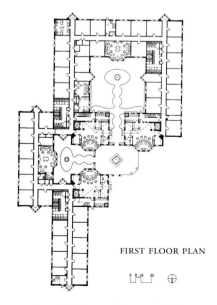

FIRST FLOOR PLAN

ABOVE: The three entrances, small in scale and domestic in image, give the complex a clarity of organization.
Photo: Robert Benson

OPPOSITE: Courtyards break up the massive size of the complex and create suntraps.
Photo: Robert Benson

*H*ouse in Central Connecticut

The additions and changes requested by the clients for their house, the plan of which was roughly based on a central-chimney colonial prototype, included a better outdoor space for entertaining, a new entry and kitchen, and larger and more pleasant bedrooms.

On the east side of the house, the architects extended the garage roof and made a pergola to create a sort of pavilion for food preparation and dining. Echoing the shape of the pavilion is a small, new screen porch adjoining the kitchen and family room. New on the south side is a terrace onto which open the living, dining, and family rooms and, to shade these rooms, a porch roof and pergola.

To shelter the previously unprotected north-facing main entrance, the designers added a new entry porch and vestibule. The new light-filled kitchen, incorporating a commercial-type range and grill and an island of counter space, enables two people to work simultaneously while being screened from the family dining room.

In second-floor bedrooms, the architects added new dormers and expanded existing rooms into attics and additions. As a result, the younger son's bedroom now includes dormer windows on two sides, the older son's room has a loft space, and the master suite at the west end of the second floor includes an exercise room, a bedroom with a fireplace and a tray ceiling, and an adjoining open porch overlooking the garden.

OPPOSITE, TOP: A new entrance porch and vestibule provide cover and shelter. The new wing on the west end of the house includes a library and master bedroom.

Photo: Robert Benson

OPPOSITE, BOTTOM: The first impression of the porch and vestibule as a traditional entrance is belied by floor-to-ceiling windows in the vestibule.

Photo: Robert Benson

LEFT: The pavilion provides a covered place for outdoor cooking. The roof of the screen porch recalls that of the pavilion without repeating it.

Photo: Robert Benson

BELOW: The living, dining, and family rooms open onto a new south terrace. A new porch roof and pergola provide needed shade and give the terrace spatial definition.

Photo: Robert Benson

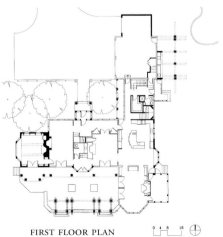

FIRST FLOOR PLAN   0 4 8   16

SECOND FLOOR PLAN   0 4 8   16

$\mathcal{M}$edia Laboratory

Massachusetts Institute of Technology
Cambridge, Massachusetts

The Media Laboratory at M.I.T. is the world's premier center for studying the interaction between computers and people. Like a school of the arts, it is a place of invention and exploration. Originally designed by I. M. Pei, the building houses three groups focusing on communication, entertainment, and education. With the Media Lab's success came a need for expansion. It was the hope of Director Nicholas Negroponte that an addition would foster interaction among these experts.

Centerbrook was engaged to fill in the unused top 15 feet of a 60-foot-high core black-box theater to create a new third-floor computer "garden" filled with ad-hoc arrangements of computers and work surfaces and ringed with glass-fronted faculty offices. Below this, the theater was given a new walk-on-wire mesh ceiling to more easily arrange lighting and speakers for productions and experiments.

While the renovations are very much in the spirit of the original building, new design elements were added to cheer on a sense of happy chaos. Surrounding the garden, the architects added brightly banded metal strips at office dividers, suggesting mysterious coding. A stainless-steel trough just below the ceiling contains ivy, bringing nature into the center of the high-tech building.

Centerbrook also renovated the second-floor director's office suite with industrial grating ceilings and custom furniture. And on the ground floor, the architects designed a ceiling mural of neon to illuminate and enliven a new social center lobby.

ABOVE: A new, flexible computer "garden" was carved out of the top 15 feet of the building's black-box theater. The space is surrounded by glass-fronted offices. Small halogen track uplights provide soft, glare-free ambient light and become focused downlights for desk tasks.

Photo: Steve Rosenthal

ABOVE: After Centerbrook lowered the ceiling of the Media Lab's Bartos black-box theater and removed a moving crane, they designed a walk-on tensile grid to allow easy preparation for a multiplicity of uses. Here the theater was set up as a computer garden for the Media Lab's 10/10 Celebration, "A Day in the Life" and became the hub of a world e-mail-in.

Photo: Steve Rosenthal

LEFT: The new, lower ceiling of the black-box theater has a walk-on grid of tensioned stainless cables for easy placement of lighting and sound equipment.
Photo: Steve Rosenthal

OPPOSITE: The director's office has a table custom designed by Centerbrook with sandblasted stainless steel legs and a hidden communications core. Industrial grating is hung from the ceiling with lighting above, casting theatrical shadows in the space.
Photo: Steve Rosenthal

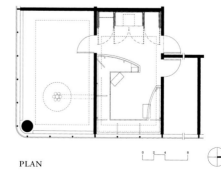

PLAN

ABOVE RIGHT: The reception room has new built in furniture, including a glass-walled coffee bar and work stations.
Photo: Steve Rosenthal

RIGHT, BOTTOM: New neon strips in an abstract pattern enliven the previously dark first-floor lobby.
Photo: Steve Rosenthal

𝒲estern Maryland College

ABOVE: Centerbrook replaced the attic doors in The Studio with an insulated window and opened the ceiling to bring in natural light.
Photo: Jeff Goldberg/Esto

LEFT: In Alumni Hall new stairway railings and balusters match the originals. A new wheelchair lift provides access to the orchestra level.
Photo: Jeff Goldberg/Esto

OPPOSITE: New circular case-study classrooms in Hill Hall contain state-of-the-art computer and video projection technology while retaining historic paneling and windows.
Photo: Jeff Goldberg/Esto

Western Maryland College is set on a hilltop in a small town not far from Washington, DC. The college's setting was designed by the landscape architecture firm of Frederick Law Olmsted; its buildings represent most types of collegiate architecture from the Civil War to the present.

The college originally hired Centerbrook to design an addition to Lewis Hall, a science building with original lab benches and mechanical systems from 1910. While fundraising for the addition was in progress, Centerbrook renovated six other buildings. One was Peterson Hall.

The college asked Centerbrook to bring back, as much as possible, this three-story building's earlier details, making it fully accessible to the handicapped, and restoring its exterior. The designers made the third floor into a gallery for the college's permanent art collection. On the ground floor they added a new computer graphics studio, design studios, and a faculty office. The architects uncovered and restored many buried interior details throughout the building.

Memorial Hall (now called Hill Hall) began as the college's science building. Centerbrook renovated the top two floors into offices for faculty, the ground floor into classrooms, and the first or main floor into two large case-study lecture rooms, a writing classroom, and two large seminar rooms.

The architects also cleaned and repaired the exterior of the building, restoring original oak paneling, doors, and trim.

Alumni Hall is the college's principal auditorium and theater. Centerbrook developed a cost-effective combination of an outdoor ramp and an indoor wheelchair lift, while matching the existing exterior and interior materials.

Centerbrook's renovation of The Studio turned a garage into a new ceramics studio, and introduced a high window into a drawing and painting studio.

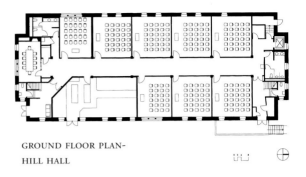

GROUND FLOOR PLAN-
HILL HALL

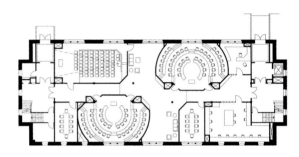

FIRST FLOOR PLAN-
HILL HALL

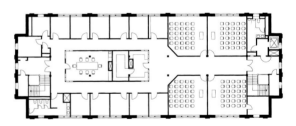

SECOND FLOOR PLAN-
HILL HALL

BELOW: New tin ceilings and oak paneling that match the originals add to the historic character of Hill Hall.
Photo: Jeff Goldberg/Esto

OPPOSITE: Careful demolition of Peterson's top floor studios revealed original architectural details, which Centerbrook restored. It uncovered the original skylight and transformed the former library stacks into a gallery for the college's permanent collection and special exhibitions.
Photo: Jeff Goldberg/Esto

GROUND FLOOR PLAN-
PETERSON

FIRST FLOOR PLAN-
PETERSON

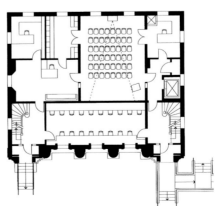

SECOND FLOOR PLAN-
PETERSON

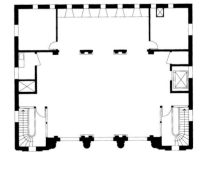

Shaw's Cove Medical Arts Building

ABOVE: All reception and waiting areas are located near windows or skylights to reduce patients' anxiety and claustrophobia.
Photo: Robert Benson

OPPOSITE: The new lobby provides a pleasant sitting area for patients awaiting transportation.
Photo: Robert Benson

When the late-1980s boom in speculative office buildings was over in New London, Connecticut, there were bargains to be had by buying foreclosed properties. Six young doctors seized the opportunity to purchase and renovate one building for their own offices and two more to rent to others.

The structure and skin of the Shaw's Cove building were in reasonably good shape, but the principal entrance was unpleasant and the offices were unsuitable for physicians' use. The clients asked Centerbrook to design a new entrance atrium and suites for eight medical practices.

Because much of the experience of seeing a doctor involves anxious waiting, Centerbrook's design focused on making the wait less distressing by locating waiting rooms and doctor's offices on outside walls near windows; examining rooms, which require more privacy, are located toward the interior. The designers scaled and proportioned all spaces to be comfortable but not claustrophobic. The pediatric practice contains a play space, and the optometrist's waiting area includes a shopping area for eyeglasses and frames. The outdoors is visible from every area where patients are required to wait, and children are provided with toys and small-scale play areas.

Restricting cost was very important to the doctors and their bankers. The architects achieved economies by reusing existing mechanical systems and by using standardized casework and finishes for examining rooms and standardized trim and finish details. Centerbrook incorporated the ideas of every doctor and his staff into a design concept that allowed each practice a degree of diversity within a coherent overall scheme. Doctors could select from a variety of economical but interesting floor coverings, wall colors, furniture, casework materials, and other finishes. It was a case of severe constraints producing interesting and innovative solutions.

FIRST FLOOR PLAN

SECOND FLOOR PLAN

The O'Connell House

The client, a plastic surgeon, asked Centerbrook to design a face lift for his house, to enlarge (on a very tight lot) a two-car garage into a four-car structure, and to create a small media room in an unused attic over the garage.

The facelift included a new wood-shingle roof, new trim and columns for the porches on the north and south sides of the house, and new muntins that change the scale of existing windows. The treatment of the porch facing the street is restrained and neighborly; the design of the porches facing the water, which are seen from a public road several hundred yards to the south, remains respectful, despite their larger scale.

The garage was enlarged, without overwhelming the lot or the neighborhood, in part by deepening it so that the cars could be placed in tandem. An existing north-facing dormer was doubled in size to bring light and views into the media room.

LEFT: The new entry porch is restrained and neighborly; an enlarged dormer brings daylight to new rooms on the second floor

Photo: Robert Benson

THIS PAGE, CLOCKWISE FROM TOP: Columns and trim on porches facing the water were scaled, in part, with the view in mind.

Photo: Robert Benson

The renovated porches frame views of the water.

Photo: Robert Benson

The south elevation of the O'Connell residence, as seen from across the marsh.

Photo: Robert Benson

School of Law Center

The 130,000-square-foot law school center forms the west terminus of the college's "village street," established in Centerbrook's 1979 campus master plan. The architects accommodated the scale of this large complex to that of the rest of the campus by dividing the center into four wings and keeping it to two stories above grade. They placed one level of the library below ground and brought in daylight through a ten-foot-wide glass roof that follows along the entire perimeter of the library wing.

The complex's principal organizing feature is a central courtyard. The main interior hallway edges the courtyard, giving the building a clear and memorable organization. The court is graced with cafe tables, chairs, benches, blossoming shade trees, and a large lawn. On a symbolic and functional level, the courtyard provides a forum for public life, a courthouse square, in effect.

Twin spires and a clock tower further distinguish the courtyard. The east spire serves as a landmark identifying the main entrance from both the courtyard to the south and the driveway to the north. The spires, whose interior arches and intersecting barrel vaults take their inspiration from Sir Christopher Wren's masterpiece, the church of St. Stephen of Wolbrook in London, are intended to lift the students' spirits and thoughts. The complex's overall "sociability"—its places to sit on the edge of paths, its enclaves for gatherings, its small indoor and outdoor cafes—all speak to "the central purpose of the practice of law and of the school itself, that of bringing people together," according to Jeff Riley.

ABOVE: The east tower, marking the main entrance, can be approached from two sides. A separate outdoor entrance to the lower-level law clinic offers privacy.
Photo: Jeff Goldberg/Esto

OPPOSITE: The School of Law Center's large size is broken up into four wings.
Photo: Jeff Goldberg/Esto

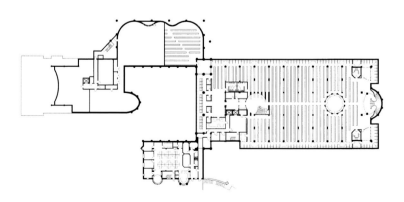

LOWER PLAN

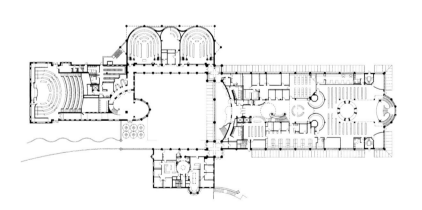

MAIN FLOOR PLAN

RIGHT: The courtyard provides a "forum for public life." Marking the main entrance is the east tower.
Photo: Jeff Goldberg/Esto

BELOW LEFT: Light monitors are located over indoor sitting areas.
Photo: Jeff Goldberg/Esto

BELOW RIGHT: The west tower's balcony overlooks the main entry lobby.
Photo: Jeff Goldberg/Esto

OPPOSITE: The center forms the western terminus of the campus' "village street."
Photo: Jeff Goldberg/Esto

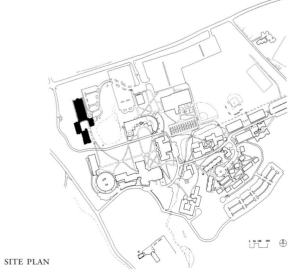

SITE PLAN

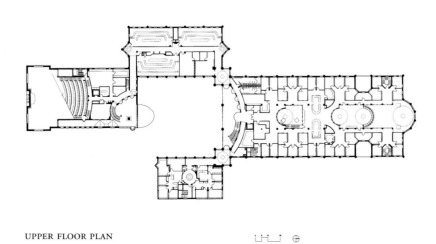

UPPER FLOOR PLAN

THIS PAGE, CLOCKWISE FROM
TOP: Classrooms are equipped
with multi-sync monitors and
seating in the round for inter-
active learning.
Photo: Jeff Goldberg/Esto

A view of the courtyard and
the library skylights from the
east tower.
Photo: Jeff Goldberg/Esto

The faculty lounge provides
a forum for discussing disserta-
tions, articles, and books in
progress.
Photo: Jeff Goldberg/Esto

THIS PAGE, CLOCKWISE FROM TOP: Skylights at grade level introduce daylight into the subterranean level of the library.
Photo: Jeff Goldberg/Esto

The cite-check room for the Law Review is located within the library.
Photo: Jeff Goldberg/Esto

Study carrels are arranged beneath a skylight that follows the entire perimeter of the library's lower level.
Photo: Jeff Goldberg/Esto

LEFT: The ceiling of the moot court is made of mahogany plywood panels that are spaced four inches apart and have sound-absorbing insulation above.

Photo: Jeff Goldberg/Esto

BOTTOM: Reading balconies overlook the student cafe.

Photo: Jeff Goldberg/Esto

OPPOSITE: The moot court room doubles as a classroom. A sounding board above the judge's bench, combined with sound-deadening panels used as backing for auditorium seating, makes for excellent acoustics.

Photo: Jeff Goldberg/Esto

THIS PAGE, CLOCKWISE FROM TOP: Reading areas are dispersed among the library stacks.
Photo: Jeff Goldberg/Esto

The reference desk is the library's central focus. Near it, a stair leads to the faculty offices and conveniently passes by the circulation desk.
Photo: Jeff Goldberg/Esto

The main entry lobby brings the outdoors inside.
Photo: Jeff Goldberg/Esto

The rotunda at the north end of the library offers lounge seating with a panoramic view of Sleeping Giant Mountain.
Photo: Jeff Goldberg/Esto

OPPOSITE: The vaults of the two towers were inspired by Sir Christopher Wren's St. Stephen of Wolbrook Church in London.
Photo: Jeff Goldberg/Esto

$\mathcal{F}$ood Science Research Laboratory

Pfizer, Incorporated
Groton, Connecticut

This 8,000-square-foot addition to a food-science research laboratory is located on a pharmaceutical research campus. The completed building functions as the worldwide technical center for the company's food science research and development activities. The program's principal requirement was a large new teleconferencing space for serving client companies and coordinating operations around the world.

A new entrance brings clients and employees through a foyer with splayed walls displaying company products. An inner lobby, centered on the foyer, is the same oval shape as the company's logo. The lobby's warm-colored walls and floors contrast with a reception desk surmounted by neon lighting.

At the center of the addition is the large teleconferencing room. Entered through doors in the lobby's curving wall on either side of the reception desk, the teleconferencing room is a big rectangular space with a large light monitor and is designed to television studio standards. The warm grey fabric wall coverings over acoustic panels provide excellent broadcast definition. The conference table is a warm color that reflects a flattering light onto the faces of participants.

The room's lights can be dimmed and have the appropriate color temperature for television broadcasts. The lights are mounted over the conference table on a truss and are programmed with automatic presets. A roof monitor admits natural light but controls it by means of deep overhangs and automated shades.

The conference table is splayed into a "stealth" shape so that participants are visible by the room's camera, which is centered between two five-foot monitors at the wide end of the table. Microphones are inset into the table, and lighting controls for the room are contained in a portable panel. A kitchen adjacent to the teleconferencing room is used for food science presentations.

OPPOSITE: The wide end of the conference table faces two five-foot screens flanking a broadcast camera (behind the sliding panel). Automated shades allow natural light from the monitor to be blocked.
Photo: Jeff Goldberg/Esto

RIGHT: Visitors enter a minimalist lobby having the oval shape of the company's logo.
Photo: Jeff Goldberg/Esto

SITE PLAN

0 10 20   40

ABOVE: The building's lobby is expressed on its exterior by an oval steel canopy over the entrance.

Photo: Jeff Goldberg/Esto

RIGHT: The company logo is mounted over the entry canopy.

Photo: Jeff Goldberg/Esto

OPPOSITE: The conference table is splayed into a "stealth" shape so that participants' faces may be viewed by the room's broadcast camera, which is set into the wall at the wide end of the table. A roof monitor mixes natural with artificial light.

Photo: Jeff Goldberg/Esto

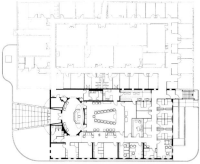

FIRST FLOOR PLAN

*U*rban Garden

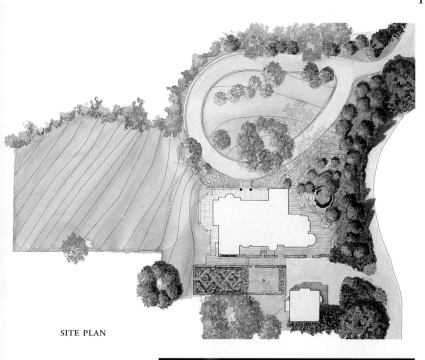

SITE PLAN

This garden surrounds a recently renovated house, originally built in 1880 in the Gothic style. Once the center of a large estate, the residence is now surrounded by an urban area. Centerbrook worked with landscape architect Lester Collins to create a garden that provides an escape from the city, while contributing to the landscape of the neighborhood.

A terraced path around the large house connects several gardens—a favorite device of Collins's—and allows children on bicycles and adults on foot to easily explore the landscape. Each garden takes advantage of the natural terrain.

The entrance to the house is from the north and is dominated by the canopy of a 300-year-old oak tree. The lawn and driveway were refurbished and a weeping hemlock was carefully sited at the drive's entrance to create an open and welcoming entrance to the house.

Narrow stone steps from the driveway lead to the east garden, which takes advantage of a rugged rock outcropping. The rock has been exposed and the crevices planted with flowers to create a colorful view from the kitchen. A gothic terrace in the rock has a stone floor modeled after the floor of Amiens Cathedral. This garden provides a protected place for children to play.

The terraced path from the east garden steps down between stone walls planted with flowers to the south garden, designed as an outdoor room bordered by flower walls and gothic trellises. In the center is an old stone grist wheel that has been turned into a fountain. A formal perennial garden is found nearby by wandering through a gothic trellis.

Beyond the south garden, the terraced path leads to a grand porch on the house's west and north sides. The west porch overlooks a large lawn that has been sculpted to provide views to the river below. The owners share this lawn with the neighborhood; it is ideal for sledding in the winter and watching the sun set year-round.

OPPOSITE: The fountain is made from a grist wheel found on-site. The sound of water masks the noise of the surrounding city.
Photo: Jeff Goldberg/Esto

THIS PAGE, CLOCKWISE FROM TOP: The new trellis, covered in clematis, carries the Gothic character of the house into the garden.
Photo: Jeff Goldberg/Esto

A path lined with flower walls leads past an outdoor room to the front lawn. Overlooked by a majestic magnolia tree, the room provides a place of tranquility.
Photo: Jeff Goldberg/Esto

The Gothic terrace in the east garden is set on a rugged outcropping of rock.
Photo: Jeff Goldberg/Esto

$\mathcal{P}$omfret School

Pomfret, Connecticut

ABOVE: The entry has two cast columns with bronze capitals recalling the school's first 100 years.

Photo: Steve Rosenthal

OPPOSITE: The Centennial building is located below the original school building on the site of the smaller Pyne Dormitory, which was moved across campus. The Centennial aligns with other campus buildings and follows their lead in materials and character.

Photo: Steve Rosenthal

Pomfret School is a highly respected prep school offering rigorous academics and a special focus on the arts. In observation of its 100th anniversary, and in response to its recent growth to three hundred students, the school commissioned the new Centennial Academic and Arts Center. This 20,000-square-foot building would include painting and sculpture studios; carpentry, metal, and welding shops; fourteen classrooms; and a 125-seat auditorium.

The campus plan designed by Ernest Flagg, the turn-of-the-century Beaux Arts architect, had been abandoned during recent campus additions. By moving Flagg's Pyne Dormitory and positioning the new Centennial building on an axis with the original four-story school building by Flagg, the architects re-established the principles of quadrangles and axes from the original plan. They moved Pyne Dormitory—a brick-and-slate structure weighing more than five hundred tons—more than seven hundred feet, and renovated it to house two faculty families and sixteen students.

The Centennial Academic and Arts Center sits on a hill that slopes to the west, allowing an on-grade entry on two levels. Occupying the lowest floor are shops and an auditorium that are easily accessible from a campus road. Finishes are simple; ceilings are exposed.

Fourteen classrooms and three seminar rooms occupy the two upper floors. Most important to the design of classrooms was that they be large and have strategically placed teachers' desks. It was the intention that each room would be home for a year to a single teacher who could create unique class layouts and learning environments.

At the center of the building, behind the front doors and facing the quad, is an oval entry called the "Fauxtunda" in honor of its shallow, domelike ceiling dramatized by a corona of painted boards.

RIGHT, TOP: The building's twin wings embrace a central entryway to reflect the rhyming and twinning found in the original campus buildings by Ernest Flagg. The wings also suggest the double use of the building, for arts and academics.
Photo: Steve Rosenthal

BELOW: The wings align with porticoes on either side of the building and can be seen from the front yard of the campus.
Photo: Steve Rosenthal

OPPOSITE: The main entry hall, the "Fauxtunda," is a shallow oval suggesting a grand space in what is a widened corridor.
Photo: Steve Rosenthal

CLOCKWISE FROM TOP: The painting studio has a high ceiling with skylights at the ridge to bounce northern light onto the main wall.

Photo: Steve Rosenthal

The lecture room on the ground floor doubles as a black box theater complete with a control room and pipe grid for lighting.

Photo: Steve Rosenthal

Most classrooms have niches for teachers' offices. The school envisioned classrooms personalized by individual teachers to suit their teaching style.

Photo: Steve Rosenthal

CENTENNIAL
BASEMENT PLAN   0 5 10   20

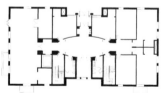

CENTENNIAL
FIRST FLOOR PLAN   0 5 10   20

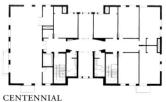

CENTENNIAL
SECOND FLOOR PLAN   0 5 10   20

LEFT: Once the school infirmary, Pomfret School moved Pyne Dormitory seven hundred feet and transformed it into a dormitory housing sixteen students and two faculty families. New fire stairs were carved out of the building at each end and the entry was moved from the end of the building to its side, yet the only additions to the exterior were the white portico and the chimneys.

Photo: Steve Rosenthal

BELOW: With an efficiently used volume, some of Pyne Dormitory's rooms tuck under the eaves, fitting many residents comfortably into what looks like a small building.

Photo: Steve Rosenthal

PYNE DORMITORY
FIRST FLOOR PLAN

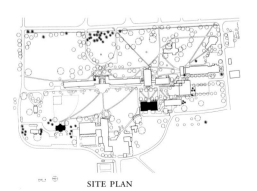

SITE PLAN

Kitchings House

The architect's charge was to renovate and add to a contemporary house built in the early 1970s. The clients, a family of five, loved the site but wanted the house changed in many ways, not the least of which was to make it more traditional. The design approach was to add a gable roof to the flat-roofed garage and a new bedroom wing and pool house to make a "village" of buildings surrounding a forecourt that replaces a circular driveway. The result is to make the house appear less modern and integrate its living spaces with the landscape. Also helpful was removal of overgrown trees and bushes, which now gives the house expansive views of a nearby cove and salt marsh.

To further reduce the scale of the complex, the designers selected different colors for different elements. The look of incremental additions recalls houses in Maine connected to farm buildings, gradually expanded by different owners. The Kitchings' house now expresses a broad mixture of architectural ideas that makes the dwelling a better fit with its neighborhood and with its new owners' wishes.

ABOVE: Outbuildings encircle the vehicle courtyard.
Photo: Jeff Goldberg/Esto

RIGHT: Exterior insulation allows rafters to be exposed in the master bedroom.
Photo: Robert Benson

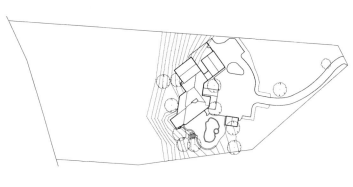

SITE PLAN   0 10 20 40

LEFT: The terrace is made of Stony Creek granite.
Photo: Jeff Goldberg/Esto

BELOW: The use of multiple colors reduces the apparent size of the house.
Photo: Jeff Goldberg/Esto

FIRST FLOOR PLAN

SECOND FLOOR PLAN

Guyott House

ABOVE: The house, narrow and low on the ends, stretches to capture views of a marsh and the sea on its far side.
Photo: Jeff Goldberg/Esto

OPPOSITE: The seaside elevation of the house is protected by granite and riprap walls that surround a small pool and upper-level terraces.
Photo: Jeff Goldberg/Esto

Occupying a rocky outcropping between Long Island Sound and a bird-inhabited marsh surrounding abandoned granite quarries, the Guyott House ends a road of Stick-style Victorian summer houses long ago renovated for year-round use. The owners, a retired couple, wanted a substantial house, although the lot is tight and has wetland setbacks front and back.

The garage opens at the lower grade. Enticing visitors to the main door, a floor above, are stone steps that cascade downward under an arcade with Gothic arches. These mimic the Stick-style house nearby, while the house is shingled like neighbors in the other direction. The arches of the arcade reappear as giant windows that take advantage of the wonderful views.

Local pink granite was used for site walls and steps, which on the sea side surround a plunge pool just above the beach and then step upward to terraces. The designers laid the stone in horizontal bands with deep reveals to reinforce their massiveness.

Indoors, the owners asked for spacious, unique spaces with high ceilings and fine materials, and they listed among their needs a living room, dining room, eat-in kitchen, study, poolroom, and two guest rooms.

A wide front door leads to an entry hall and a visitor's first view of the sea. Just to the left are a pair of sandblasted rolling glass doors leading to the wallpapered dining room. A winding hall leads past the kitchen where a giant, figured granite counter covers an island with a stainless lobster-pot rack hanging above it.

A few steps past the arch, up three treads, is the two-story living room. Covering one wall is a towering granite chimney facing a great 18-foot window and the sea. Overhead glass lamps hang as though dripping from bracketing. On either side of the huge window are two parrot-cage niches. The painted walls are paneled to conceal a television and audio center.

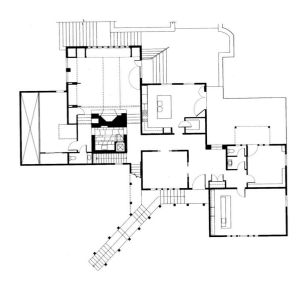

FIRST FLOOR PLAN

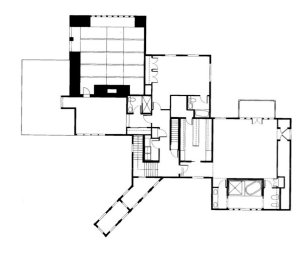

SECOND FLOOR PLAN

RIGHT: The house occupies a rock outcropping, where mosses and lichens were carefully preserved during construction.

Photo: Jeff Goldberg/Esto

ABOVE: The entry steps closely follow the bedrock.
Photo: Jeff Goldberg/Esto

RIGHT: An arched portico covers granite and bluestone steps to the front door, which is on the second level.
Photo: Jeff Goldberg/Esto

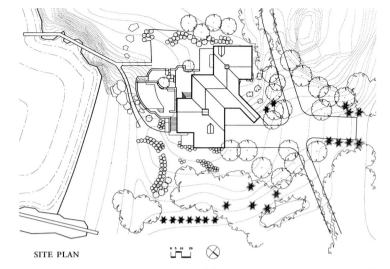

ABOVE: The dining room's sandblasted sliding doors repeat riverine patterns from the wallpaper. A light fixture designed by the architects undulates over the dining table.
Photo: Jeff Goldberg/Esto

RIGHT: The fireplace and chimney are made from three types of stone: local pink granite, lilac bluestone, and soapstone in the firebox.
Photo: Jeff Goldberg/Esto

OPPOSITE: The pool has a grotto catching water from above. The stone wall is low, allowing views from one body of water to another.
Photo: Jeff Goldberg/Esto

RIGHT: Hidden behind the fireplace is a mirror-lined bar, inspired by a tomb from *Raiders of the Lost Ark.*
Photo: Jeff Goldberg/Esto

BELOW: The pool room is panelled in mahogany; its light fixture was designed by the architects.
Photo: Jeff Goldberg/Esto

OPPOSITE: The large living-room window overlooks the sea. The ceiling features bracketing and light fixtures.
Photo: Jeff Goldberg/Esto

$\mathcal{N}$orton Museum of Art

Phase I of Centerbrook's addition to the Norton Museum of Art in West Palm Beach, which was completed in late 1995, renovated the museum's existing galleries and added a new south-facing wing. The wing contains the museum's principal new entrance, a great hall entry space, visitors' services, and a high-ceilinged gallery. It faces a new entry drive that provides convenient parking for the area's significant elderly population. Phase II, which will open in late 1996, will complete the museum's expansion from 30,000 to 80,000 square feet.

The Norton was built in 1941, a period already considered historic in Florida. It was constructed in the Art Moderne style and configured as a Roman villa around an outdoor atrium. The principal entrance faced east, towards the resort community of Palm Beach.

Centerbrook's scheme retains the Norton's historic east wing but incorporates the remaining three facades, the recipients of numerous additions over the years, within a new building. While respecting the old, the new structure has contrasting flush details and more vivid colors. Its new south-facing entrance, which takes a cue from the original octagonal entrance lobby, underscores the Norton's intention to serve the entire metropolitan population and, indeed, all of South Florida. A four-story tower to be added on the north side during Phase II will make the building a gateway marking an important entrance route to downtown West Palm Beach.

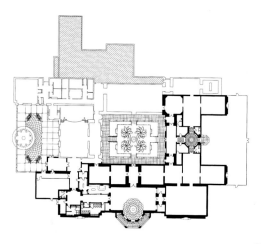

FIRST FLOOR PLAN

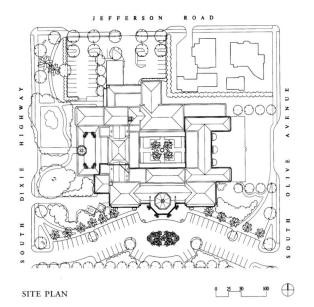

SITE PLAN

0 25 50 100

ABOVE: The new south-facing entrance takes its cue from the octagonal shape of the original lobby.
Photo: Kim Sargent

LEFT: Renovated existing galleries have new wall panels.
Photo: Kim Sargent

OPPOSITE: On the interior, the entrance pavilion's octagonal shape is expressed with clean lines.
Photo: Kim Sargent

ℱurniture, Fountains, Fixtures

I

Centerbrook is frequently asked to go beyond the strict limits of architectural design. The needs and dreams of its clients often encompass a building and its contents as well. When the budget allows—or at times demands—the architects find themselves designing a wide array of items, including furniture, light fixtures, fountains, murals, wallpaper, carpets, mosaics, fireplace utensils, sculpture, special ornaments, and even birdhouses, all to fortify a sense of place and their clients' vision.

The high degree of craft required and the comparatively small scale of these objects offer Centerbrook a proving ground for adventurous design, and an affordable way to have a lot of fun. The firm's furniture design starts with an understanding of the human body's anatomy and an eye to physical comfort. Often, furnishings reproduce or recall the design motifs of the host building. In some cases, furniture or decorative objects create or reinforce a particular image or message and thus act as symbols. Exterior elements such as fountains, rain gutters, or bird-baths frequently play with the whimsy of the weather or site. Altogether, the contents of Centerbrook's buildings, their furnishings and decorative art, have a striking individual spirit, while being harmonious with their setting.

2

3

4

5

1: A fountain at the Wriston Art Center in Wisconsin, made from the end of a stainless steel beer vat, spouts steam in winter creating an ice sculpture that melts in spring.

Designer: Jefferson B. Riley

Fabricator: Thermal Electron of Wisconsin

Photographer: Paul Warchol

2: "Eidolon," the ghost made of dimmed multicolored neon, is affixed to draped translucent fabric and suspended on invisible wires.

Designer: William H. Grover

Fabricator: William H. Grover

Photographer: William H. Grover

3: "Pseudo-chandeliers" are glass sheets suspended below recessed downlights. The glass is sandblasted in patterns taken from gel-electrophoresis plates used in protein visualization. These are recognizable to scientists who use the room.

Designer: William H. Grover

Fabricator: TSAO Lighting

Photographer: Timothy Hursley

4: "Slice of Light," a white neon tube encased in stretch fabric and suspended on invisible wires.

Designers: William H. Grover and James C. Childress

Fabricator: William H. Grover

Photographer: Balthazar Korab

5: Traditional lanterns become disco lights at night at the Quinnipiac College Rathskeller.

Designers: Jefferson B. Riley and Leonard J. Wyeth with William Warfel of Systems Design Associates

Fabricator: A. W. Pistol, Inc.

Photographer: Robert Benson

6: Hand-painted fish dive over the fireplace in a house on Cape Cod.
Designer: Jefferson B. Riley
Fabricator: Jefferson B. Riley
Photographer: Timothy Hursley

7: Uplights reflect off the underside of stock perforated metal table tops at the Wriston Art Center.
Designer: Jefferson B. Riley
Fabricator: Breuer Metal Craftsmen
Photographer: Image Studios/
  Glen Hartjes

8: A master bed for the Reid House repeats the design motifs of the architecture.
Designer: Jefferson B. Riley
Fabricator: Robert Feher
Photographer: Peter Mauss/Esto

9: A side table for the Reid House uses the details of the fireplace.
Designer: Jefferson B. Riley
Fabricator: Tim Yoder of Roman Yoder
  & Sons
Photographer: Peter Mauss/Esto

10: The earth, water, and fire sculpture creates "white noise" at Rensselaer Polytechnic Institute library.
Designers: Jefferson B. Riley and
  William H. Grover
Photographer: Norman McGrath

11: A bench for the Wriston Art Center Gallery reflects the curved shape of the building's amphitheater.
Designer: Jefferson B. Riley
Fabricator: Oscar J. Boldt
  Construction Company
Photographer: Jefferson B. Riley

6

7

8

9

10

11

13

13

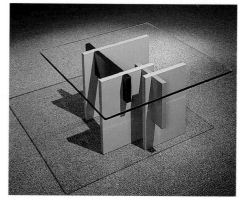

14

12: A side table for Brandeis University with a painted base and mahogany top.

Designer: Mark Simon
Fabricator: Breakfast Woodworks
Photographer: Steve Rosenthal

13: A side table with lamp for Brandeis University with a painted base, mahogany top, and Nessen lamp.

Designer: Mark Simon
Fabricator: Breakfast Woodworks
Photographer: Steve Rosenthal

15

16

14: The "Boogie Woogie" coffee table for Brandeis University has a painted base and glass top.

Designer: Mark Simon
Fabricator: Breakfast Woodworks
Photographer: Steve Rosenthal

15: A coffee table and couch is made of maple and bird's-eye maple.

Designers: Mark Simon and
James C. Childress
Fabricator: Bill Murray
Photographer: Timothy Hursley

16: The Marsh Estate stair rail has an apple tree newel, maple branch balusters, and reclaimed chestnut treads.

Designers: Mark Simon and furniture
maker Daniel Mack
Fabricator: Daniel Mack
Photographer: Norman McGrath

17

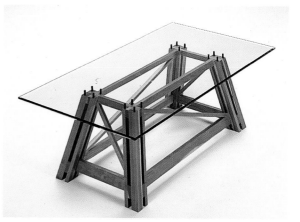

18

17: The Simon/Bellamy library ceiling uses bicycle pedal reflectors, security mirrors, road reflectors, and mirrored lenses.

Designer: Mark Simon
Fabricators: Jill Childress,
John Furness, Mark Simon
Photographer: Norman McGrath

18: The Gilbert coffee table ("Simon Table") has cherry legs and a glass top.

Designer: Mark Simon
Fabricator: Gilbert International
Photographer: Gilbert International

19: The McKim dining table uses cherry and bird's-eye maple.

Designer: Mark Simon with
　Leonard J. Wyeth

Fabricator: Bill Murray

Photographer: Timothy Hursley

20: The Marsh Estate powder room sink is made of copper plumbing and has an infrared sensor. When the room is occupied, warm water automatically runs down the gutters to the sink.

Designer: Mark Simon with
　Mahdad Saniee

Fabricator: Peter Markey Metals

Photographer: Norman McGrath

21: A five-piece floating fountain, reminiscent of the Shalimar Gardens of Kashmir, plies the waters of the Great Miami River in Dayton, Ohio.

Designers: Chad Floyd, Charles W.
　Moore, and Stephen J. Carter of
　Lorenz & Williams, Inc.

Fabricator: The Dayton Ohio
　Sheetmetal Workers Union

Photographer: Chad Floyd

22: A lamp is made of Formica Surell.

Designer: Mark Simon

Fabricator: Plexability Limited

Photographer: Barbara Karant

23: A suspended sheet of sand-blasted glass softens the glare from four halogen lamps mounted above at the Tuck School of Business Administration, Dartmouth College.

Designers: Chad Floyd and
　Susan E. Wyeth

Fabricator: Bread Loaf Construction
　Company

Photographer: Jeff Goldberg/Esto

24: The Gringer fountain is a three-inch deep wall fountain made of lead-coated copper and Heath tiles.

Designer: Mark Simon

Fabricator: Donald Gringer

Photographer: Norman McGrath

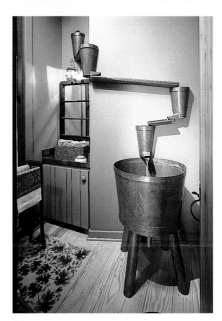
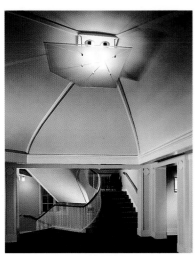

19

20

21

22

23

24

25

27

30

26

29

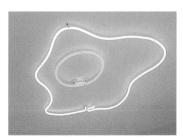

28

25: A wooden chandelier in a residential foyer can be lowered as much as twenty feet to light a holiday dining table.
Designers: Chad Floyd and
  Kevin Henson
Fabricator: Bogaert Construction
Photographer: Jeff Goldberg/Esto

26: Cocteau-inspired torches light the staircase of the Hood Museum of Art at Dartmouth College.
Designers: Chad Floyd and
  Charles W. Moore
Fabricator: Jackson Construction
Photographer: Steve Rosenthal

27: A leaded glass window is an abstraction of the floor plan of the house.
Designer: Steven J. Lloyd
Fabricator: Cathy Lovell
Photographer: Norman McGrath

28: A copper model of an adenovirus molecule tops the gazebo on the waste water treatment plant at Cold Spring Harbor Laboratory.
Designer: William H. Grover
Fabricator: William H. Grover
Photographer: Norman McGrath

29: A sharp-edged house provides a home for birds of prey.
Designer: William H. Grover
Fabricator: William H. Grover
Photographer: Margaret Wazuka

30: The image of "breakfast" rendered in neon on the wall of a breakfast nook.
Designer: William H. Grover
Fabricator: Jo-Ran Neon
Photographer: William H. Grover

31: A watercolor of a silver-plated horn reflects images of the Quinnipiac College library. The painting hangs in the college's music listening room.
Designer: William H. Grover
Artist: William H. Grover
Photographer: Jeff Goldberg/Esto

32: A couch for the Reid House recalls the curved shapes that appear elsewhere in the house.
Designer: Jefferson B. Riley
Fabricator: Nap Brothers
Photographer: Peter Mauss/Esto

33: Limestone benches at the Agora of the Quinnipiac College Student Center are stylized "roots of symbolic trees."
Designer: Jefferson B. Riley
Fabricator: Bybee Stone Company, Inc.
Photographer: Jeff Goldberg/Esto

34: A stuccoed solar-heat storage wall at the Elliott House is decorated with imprints of oak leaves and designs etched with a rake.
Designer: Jefferson B. Riley
Fabricators: Jefferson B. Riley and Anne Elliott
Photographer: Jefferson B. Riley

35: Hand-stenciled, computer-generated graphics decorate the Quinnipiac College Computer Center.
Designer: William H. Grover
Fabricator: Leonard J. Wyeth
Photographer: Norman McGrath

36: A rain fan for the Shattuck House creates visual delight.
Designer: Jefferson B. Riley
Fabricator: Richard Riggio & Sons, Inc.
Photographer: Norman McGrath

37: A table relates to a larger Prairie-style dining table.
Designer/Fabricator: Robert L. Harper
Photographer: Robert Benson

31

32

33

34

35

36

37

38

39

40

41

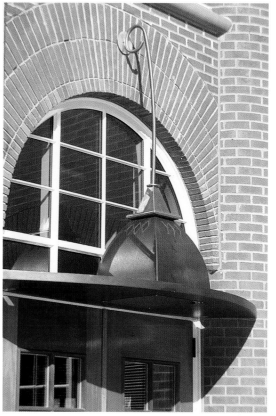

42

38: A standing lamp provides an on-line computer hook-up at the Quinnipiac College School of Law.

Designers: Jefferson B. Riley and William Warfel of Systems Design Associates

Fabricator: Valley City Manufacturing Company Limited

Photographer: Jeff Goldberg/Esto

39: Large side panels and side-mounted light fixtures provide private, glare-free study carrels at the Quinnipiac College School of Law.

Designers: Jefferson B. Riley and William Warfel of Systems Design Associates

Fabricator: Valley City Manufacturing Company Limited

Photographer: Jeff Goldberg/Esto

40: A study table with standing lamps makes four small "rooms" for two at the Quinnipiac College School of Law.

Designer: Jefferson B. Riley

Fabricator: Valley City Manufacturing Company Limited

Photographer: Jeff Goldberg/Esto

41: The legs of a team study room table at the Quinnipiac College School of Law cover floor outlets for computer hook-ups.

Designer: Jefferson B. Riley

Fabricator: BKM Woodworking Division

Photographer: Jeff Goldberg/Esto

42: An entry lamp provides a roof over a door at the Quinnipiac College School of Law.

Designer: Jefferson B. Riley

Fabricator: New England Boatworks

Photographer: Jeff Goldberg/Esto

43: Lanterns hang in the lobby of the Quinnipiac College School of Law.

Designers: Jefferson B. Riley and William Warfel of Systems Design Associates

Fabricator: A. W. Pistol, Inc.

Photographer: Jeff Goldberg/Esto

44: A magazine table at the Quinnipiac College School of Law is built to be sturdy.

Designer: Jefferson B. Riley

Fabricator: BKM Woodworking Division

Photographer: Jeff Goldberg/Esto

45: A chandelier for the Quinnipiac College School of Law has fritted glass that filters the sunlight from a dome above.

Designers: Jefferson B. Riley and William Warfel of Systems Design Associates

Fabricator: A. W. Pistol Inc.

Photographer: Jeff Goldberg/Esto

46: "Book cover" wall sconces at the Quinnipiac College School of Law have famous quotes sandblasted on glass panels.

Designers: Jefferson B. Riley and William Warfel of Systems Design Associates

Fabricator: A. W. Pistol Inc.

Photographer: Jeff Goldberg/Esto

47: The conference room coat rack at the Shapiro Admissions Center, Brandeis University, resembles a constructivist sculpture. It is made economically from simple straight sticks and boards, screwed together and painted.

Designer: Mark Simon

Fabricator: Breakfast Woodworks

Photographer: Steve Rosenthal

48: Auditorium seats at he Quinnipiac College School of Law provide writing tablets stored on the front wall.

Designer: Jefferson B. Riley

Fabricator: Valley City Manufacturing Company Limited

Photographer: Jeff Goldberg/Esto

43

44

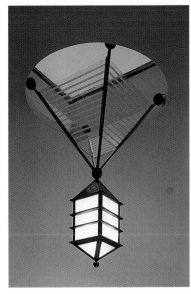

45

46

47

48

49

50

51

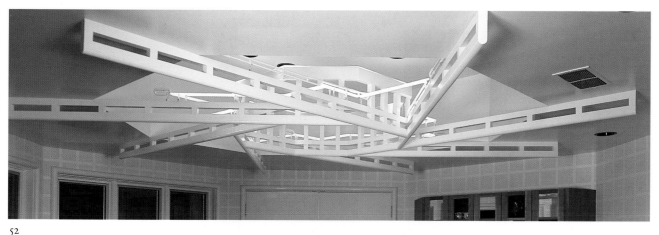

52

53

54

49: William Morris' wallpaper pattern of willow leaves is delicately sandblasted onto French doors leading to an apartment dining room.

Designer: Mark Simon
Fabricator: Donald Gringer
Photographer: Norman McGrath

50: A glass-topped table is etched with a handless clock dial.

Designer: Mark Simon
Fabricator: Donald Gringer
Photographer: Norman McGrath

51: A sconce, hinged for easy changes, shields two incandescent bulbs with a custom-slumped frosted glass shade.

Designer: Mark Simon
Fabricator: R. Bruce Laughlin of
    Creative Endeavors Inc.
Photographer: Margaret Wazuka

52: A coffered octagonal dining room is lit by a star of pink and orange neon above lattice boards.

Designer: Mark Simon
Fabricator: Crowell & Baker
Photographer: Norman McGrath

53: Signage for the Clocktower shops in Middletown, Connecticut, has layers of letters, backgrounds, and lighting.

Designers: Mark Simon and Mary
    Ann Rumney of Rumney Associates
Fabricator: Wernert Construction and
    Sign Lite
Photographer: Paul Warchol

54: A custom light combines a standard "jelly jar" fixture with a fluorescent bulb and a plastic fresnel lens as an economical fixture for the National Maritime Center.

Designers: Mark Simon and William
    Warfel of Systems Design Associates
Fabricator: A. W. Pistol Inc.
Photographer: Margaret Wazuka

66: A coffee table—with magazine shelf below—strewn with wooden "leaves" to continue the woodsy theme of the room.

Designer: Jefferson B. Riley
Fabricator: Ian Ingersoll
Photographer: Norman McGrath

67: A master bed has acorn reading lamps made of bronze and colored glass.

Designers: Jefferson B. Riley and
  Charles G. Mueller
Fabricator: Ian Ingersoll and Rob Hare
Photographer: Ian Ingersoll

68: A master bedroom bureau has a pivoting mirror.

Designers: Jefferson B. Riley and
  Charles G. Mueller
Fabricators: Ian Ingersoll and
  Rob Hare
Photographer: Ian Ingersoll

69: A bunk room table stands on tiptoes.

Designer: Jefferson B. Riley
Fabricator: Ian Ingersoll
Photographer: Brian Vanden Brink

70: Bedside tables match the other custom-designed bedroom furniture.

Designers: Jefferson B. Riley and
  Charles G. Mueller
Fabricators: Ian Ingersoll and
  Rob Hare
Photographer: Ian Ingersoll

66

67

68

69

70

71

72

73

74

71: Fifteen-foot-high doors in the Norton Museum lobby have panels that are offset by brushed aluminum reveals.

Designers: Chad Floyd,
    Jean E. Smajstrla, Jonathan G. Parks,
    and Reno J. Migani, Jr.
Fabricator: Darby and Mitchell Inc.
Photographer: Kim Sargent

72: The coffee table in the Centerbrook reception room has a base made from a giant water valve that had been part of the original factory sprinkler system. The iron casting was scraped and repainted; its brass fittings were taken off for polishing. The table top is 1/2"-thick plate glass.

Designers: Mark Simon with
    Chris Todd
Fabricators: Chris Todd with
    Milton LaPlace
Photographer: Robert Benson

73: This table lamp has three legs, each a different diameter pipe, which balance under a large cylindrical shade.

Designers: Mark Simon with Rachel
    Simon of Lights Up for
    George Kovacs
Fabricator: model by Mark Simon
Photographer: Mark Simon

74: A wall sconce in the Floyd House was assembled from standard brass castings.

Designers: Chad Floyd and
    Susan E. Wyeth
Fabricator: Chad Floyd
Photographer: Robert Benson

75: These ceiling lamps started as standard milk glass "school-house" fixtures. Centerbrook personalized them with colored bands of glazes inspired by early American pottery. Beads of colored glass were melted in a kiln onto the surface of the milk glass.

Designers: Mark Simon and
    James C. Childress
Fabricator: Laurie Vogler of
    Enchanted Glassworks
Photographer: Jeff Goldberg/Esto

76: A light fixture with painted aluminum brackets that hold a sandblasted glass shade.

Designer: James C. Childress
Fabricator: Pequot Ironworks
Photographer: Robert Benson

77: Wool rug.

Designer: Jefferson B. Riley
Fabricator: Elizabeth Eakins
Photographer: Norman McGrath

78: Mosaic tile athletes dance on floor outside the locker room at the Striar Jewish Community Center.

Designer: Jefferson B. Riley
Fabricator: Kibbutz Elon, Israel
Photographer: Steve Rosenthal

75

76

77

78

79

81

80

82

79: Frog, for the stanchions of a new bridge in Willimantic, Connecticut, was inspired by a Connecticut legend.
Sculptor/Fabricator: Leo Jensen
Photographer: Robert Benson

80: A torchère made of painted steel and glass spirals mimics the double helix of DNA at the DNA Learning Center.
Designer: James C. Childress
Fabricator: Pequot Ironworks
Photographer: Jeff Goldberg/Esto

81: A handpainted watercolor lamp shade depicts the landscape of the owner's property.
Artist: William H. Grover
Fabricator: Shades of Elegance
Photographer: Norman McGrath

82: A fireplace screen and maple leaf andirons continue the "woods" theme of a house in the Hudson Valley.
Designers: Jefferson B. Riley and
    Charles G. Mueller
Fabricator: Rob Hare
Photographer: Brian Vanden Brink

Afterword

After more than thirty years in the field of computers, I find that some of my critics still snicker: "But he is only an architect." I tell them I would take the same training because architecture school taught me to ask questions, not just solve problems. What I never knew in school was that the closest I would get to practicing architecture would be as a client, which I now am for Centerbrook.

The best way to describe Centerbrook's role in the futuristic world I inhabit is to describe the future and compare it to the past by thinking about atoms and bits. Atoms we understand. We are made of them, we eat them, we wear them, and we live and work in them. Most of our laws, almost all of our trade, and much of our social behavior is driven by atoms. But this is changing. In the future, most people will get their education, earn their incomes, and spend their leisure time with bits as much, or even more, than with atoms. Bits are different. They have no size, no shape, no color, and no mass; they move at the speed of light. Humans cannot experience bits.

This means that the interface, the place where atoms and bits meet, needs very special attention and, in particular, needs to be personalized. That is where Centerbrook comes in. They know that the commonly held idea that computers should be lined up in rows is beyond contempt. Within and beyond arm's reach must be a carefully designed space, one which has humor, elegance, comfort, and flexible layers of privacy. At the MIT Media Lab, they gave us front yards, back yards and a common area we call "the pond."

Computer hackers are nocturnal people. Rush hour at the Media Lab is between midnight and 3:00 A.M. Under such conditions lighting and ornament play an even more important role than in the nine-to-five world. Color, plants, and even toys are very much part of nerd pride and are important elements at the gateway to cyberspace. The digerati are some of the most human people you will ever meet. Centerbrook decoded their peculiarities and preferences at the Lab to make lively, personal places.

Bits will change the world. They will narrow the gap between rich and poor. They are empowering, harmonizing and globalizing. But we can't eat them, we can't wear them, and we can't live in them. As our minds, self-esteem, and ability to communicate get better and better, we will expect the same of our physical environment. After all, as Centerbrook knows, the important qualities of life have more to do with atoms than bits. They reinforce my pride in being, as my critics say, "only an architect."

Nicholas Negroponte
Cambridge, Massachusetts

Project Credits

Wilson Hall (pages 14–15)
Dartmouth College
Hanover, New Hampshire
Client: Dartmouth College
Project Designer: Chad Floyd
Project Team: Richard L. King (project manager), Steven L. Lloyd, Julia Miner
Landscape Architect: Lester Collins
Consulting Engineers: Besier Gibble Norden (structural), Helenski Zimmerer (mechanical, electrical, plumbing)
Contractor: Jackson Construction

House in Rural Connecticut (pages 16–19)
Project Designers: Jefferson B. Riley and Nick Deaver
Consulting Engineers: ERG Inc. (mechanical, electrical)
Contractor: John T. Maloney

Recreation Center (pages 20–21)
Quinnipiac College
Hamden, Connecticut
Client: Quinnipiac College
Project Designers: Jefferson B. Riley and Leonard J. Wyeth
Project Team: Robert G. Proctor, Jon M. Lavy, John Simonetti, Sheryl A. Milardo, Michael J. Milne, Sheri Bryant Lucero
Landscape: Centerbrook with Michael Cegan, Richter Cegan & Webb
Consulting Engineers: Besier Gibble Norden (structural), R. G. Vanderweil Engineers (mechanical), Nathan L. Jacobson & Associates (civil)
Contractor: F.I.P. Construction, Inc.

Private Residence (pages 22–25)
Lyme, Connecticut
Project Designer: Chad Floyd
Project Team: D. Michael Hellinghausen (project manager), Stephen L. Lloyd, Howard A. Langner, Roger U. Williams, D. Randel Wilmont, Thomas A. Morton, Sheryl A. Milardo
Landscape Architect: Lester Collins
Consulting Engineers: Besier Gibble Norden (structural)
Consultants: Systems Design Associates (lighting)
Contractor: Sal Sapia Construction

Biomedical Research Laboratory (pages 26–29)
Neurogen Corporation
Branford, Connecticut
Client: Neurogen Corporation
Project Designers: William H. Grover and James A. Coan
Project Team: Roger U. Williams, Stephen B. Holmes
Consulting Engineers: Besier Gibble Norden (structural), R. G. Vanderweil Engineers (mechanical, electrical), Metcalf & Sanborn (civil)
Contractor: W. J. Barney Construction Co. (Phase I), Frank Downes Construction Co. (Phase II)

Long View (pages 30–35)
New England
Project Designers: Mark Simon with Matthew C. Conley
Project Team: D. Michael Hellinghausen, Jean E. Smajstrla, Jon M. Lavy, Charles G. Mueller, Dennis Dowd, Sheryl A. Milardo, Michael J. Milne, Kevin Henson, Robert G. Proctor, William Egan, Howard A. Langner, Rossana Santos, Howard Rosenberg, Michael Casolo, Robert Stein, David Altman
Landscape Architect: Johnson and Richter
Consulting Engineers: Besier Gibble Norden (structural), James E. Berning, P.E. (mechanical, electrical)
Contractor: Withheld at owner's request

Discovery Research Center (pages 36–41)
DeKalb Plant Genetics Corporation
Stonington, Connecticut
Client: DeKalb Plant Genetics Corporation
Project Designers: William H. Grover and Sheri Bryant Lucero
Project Team: Ida Vorum, Robert L. Harper, Roger U. Williams, Susan E. Wyeth, Michael J. Milne, Sheryl A. Milardo, Michael J. Crosbie, C. Todd Delfosse, Daniel H. Glynn, Walker J. Burns III, Jonathan G. Parks, D. Michael Hellinghausen, Jean E. Smajstrla, Matthew C. Conley, Michael Garner, Daniel M. Vickers, Stephen B. Holmes, George W. Penniman
Consulting Engineers: Besier Gibble Norden (structural), R. G. Vanderweil Engineers (mechanical, electrical), Doane Engineering (civil), Fuss & O'Neill Inc. (site, zoning)
Contractor: The Atlas Construction Company

Academic Center and Honors Housing (pages 42–45)
The University of Toledo
Toledo, Ohio
Client: The University of Toledo
Project Designers: Chad Floyd and Nick Deaver
Project Team: Michael Garner, Matthew C. Conley, Charles G. Mueller, Robert G. Proctor, Sheri Bryant Lucero, Sheryl A. Milardo
Prime Architect: Seyfang Blanchard Duket Porter: Robert F. Seyfang and Michael Duket with Kevin J. Young
Consulting Engineers: Ulrich-Chang, Inc. (structural, civil), H. T. Bernsdorff Inc. (mechanical), Nelson Gibson and Associates, Inc. (electrical)
Contractor: Rudolph/Libbe Inc.

Eisenstein House (pages 46–47)
Midwest
Client: Edward Eisenstein
Project Designers: Mark Simon and Charles G. Mueller
Project Team: C. Todd Delfosse
Consulting Engineers: Besier Gibble Norden (structural)
Contractor: Oakstone Construction

DNA Learning Center (pages 48–51)
Cold Spring Harbor Laboratory
Cold Spring Harbor, New York
Client: Cold Spring Harbor Laboratory
Project Designers: James C. Childress and Roger U. Williams
Project Team: Liam Winters
Consulting Engineers: Besier Gibble Norden (structural)
Contractor: Jack Richards, Cold Spring Harbor Laboratory

The Amos Tuck School of Business Administration (pages 52–59)
Dartmouth College
Hanover, New Hampshire
Client: Dartmouth College
Project Designers: Chad Floyd and Susan E. Wyeth
Byrne Hall Project Team: Susan E. Wyeth (project manager), D. Michael
Hellinghausen (project manager), Charles G. Mueller, Sheryl A. Milardo,
Robert G. Proctor, Craig W. Grund, Michael J. Crosbie
Stell Hall Project Team: Susan E. Wyeth (project manager), D. Michael
Hellinghausen (project manager), Charles G. Mueller, Sheryl A. Milardo
Landscape Architect: Rolland/Towers
Consulting Engineers: Besier Gibble Norden (structural),
Helenski/Zimmerer (mechanical, electrical)
Consultants: Crabtree McGrath Associates Inc. (food service), Acentech
Incorporated (audio-visual, acoustical), Dian Boone (furnishings),
Strong-Cohen (graphics), Andrew Chartwell & Company (cost),
Christine Faye (specifications)
Contractor: Bread Loaf Construction Company

McClintock Laboratory (pages 60–63)
Cold Spring Harbor Laboratory
Cold Spring Harbor, New York
Client: Cold Spring Harbor Laboratory
Project Designers: William H. Grover and Nick Deaver
Project Team: Susan E. Wyeth
Consulting Engineers: Besier Gibble Norden (structural),
R. G. Vanderweil Engineers (mechanical, electrical)
Contractor: Cold Spring Harbor Laboratory

Ridgway House (pages 64–67)
Old Lyme, Connecticut
Client: Mr. and Mrs. William C. Ridgway III
Project Designer: Robert L. Harper
Project Team: Jonathan G. Parks (project manager), Ann L. Patterson
Consulting Engineers: Besier Gibble Norden (structural)
Contractor: Post Road Wood Products, Inc.

Kwasha Lipton Offices (pages 68–71)
Fort Lee, New Jersey
Client: Kwasha Lipton
Project Designers: Mark Simon and Jean E. Smajstrla
Project Team: Peter T. Coffin, Edward J. Keagle, Reno J. Migani, Jr.,
Darin C. Cook, Daniel H. Glynn, Julia Harrison, Peter A. Van Deusen,
Jeffrey Gotta, Sheryl A. Milardo, Christopher Arelt, Jon M. Lavy, Walker

J. Burns III, Megan N. Gibson, Gregory E. Nucci, Mahdad Saniee,
David L. Huggins, Jonathan G. Parks, Robert L. Harper, John M. Doyle,
Michael J. Crosbie, Michael Garner, Stephen B. Holmes
Consulting Engineers: Besier Gibble Norden (structural), Altieri Sebor
Wieber Consulting Engineers (mechanical, electrical, plumbing)
Consultants: Cline Bettridge Bernstein (lighting), Klepper Marshall King
Associates (acoustics)
Contractor: Nova Interiors, Inc.

Lender School of Business Center (pages 72–79)
Quinnipiac College
Hamden, Connecticut
Client: Quinnipiac College
Project Designers: Jefferson B. Riley and Leonard J. Wyeth
Project Team: Michael J. Milne, Robert G. Proctor, Jon M. Lavy, James
C. Childress, John A. Simonetti, Wanmaizan Wanradzi, Sheri Bryant
Lucero, Michael J. Crosbie, Jonathan G. Parks, George W. Penniman,
Christopher J. Payne, Michael Garner, Paul L. Shainberg, Charlotte C.
Breed, Sheryl A. Milardo
Landscape: Centerbrook with Michael Cegan, Richter Cegan & Webb
Consulting Engineers: Besier Gibble Norden (structural), James E.
Berning, P.E. (mechanical, electrical), Nathan L. Jacobson & Associates
(civil)
Consultants: Hans Knutzen Associates, Inc. (television, audio-visual)
Contractor: F.I.P. Construction, Inc.

Erle House (pages 80–83)
Guilford, Connecticut
Client: Ms. Syoko Aki Erle
Project Designers: James C. Childress and Paul L. Shainberg
Project Team: Christopher Arelt, Matthew Johnson
Contractor: Triangle Builders

The National Maritime Center, Nauticus (pages 84–93)
Norfolk, Virginia
Client: The National Maritime Center Authority
Project Designers and Project Managers: Mark Simon and James A. Coan
Project Team: Charles W. Moore, Chad Floyd, James R. Martin,
Jonathan G. Parks, Wanmaizan Wanradzi, C. Todd Delfosse, Kyra Hauser
Associated Architects: Shriver & Holland Associates: Henry V. Shriver,
Partner-in-Charge; Aubrey C. Brock, Project Architect; Joseph T. Gaber,
Joseph C. Freeman, Timothy J. Bell, John W. Myers, Richard G. Poole,
John W. Hasten, Thomas B. White, William N. Bissell, Michael N. Scott,
Janet P. Kramer, Mark L. Treon, Frank H. Hitch, Kenneth E. Blankenship
Landscape Architect: Lester Collins
Consulting Engineers: Spiegel Zamecnik & Shah Inc. (structural), Altieri
Sebor Wieber Consulting Engineers (mechanical, electrical, plumbing),
Glenn & Sadler Associates, Inc. (sitework, marine), Hayes, Seay, Mattern
& Mattern, Inc. (traffic, civil), Vansant and Gusler Inc. (site mechanical,
electrical, plumbing), Mueser Rutledge Consulting Engineers (soils,
geotechnical), P.R. Sherman Inc. (fire protection, code)
Consultants: White Oak Associates Inc. (operations consultant),

Andrew Chartwell & Company (cost), Systems Design Associates (lighting), Dorfsman-Zelenko Associates Inc. (graphics), Sigma Design Group (theater design), Davy and Associates Inc. (theater acoustics), F. M. Constantino, John Blood (architectural illustrators), Environmental Models (model maker), Ken Champlin Associates (architectural model photography), Herb Rosenthal & Associates (project concept, exhibit design), Maltbie Associates (exhibit fabricator/contractor), Ralph Appelbaum Associates Inc. (exhibit planners and designers)
Contractor: W. M. Jordan Company, Inc.

Watson House (pages 94–101)
Cold Spring Harbor Laboratory
Cold Spring Harbor, New York
Client: Cold Spring Harbor Laboratory
Project Designers: William H. Grover and Mahdad Saniee
Project Team: Paul L. Shainberg, George W. Penniman
Landscape Architect: Morgan Wheelock
Consulting Engineers: Spiegel Zamecnik & Shah Inc. (structural), Cold Spring Harbor Laboratory (mechanical, electrical)
Contractor: Jack Richards and William Baldwin, Cold Spring Harbor Laboratory

Pfizer, Incorporated (pages 102–107)
Groton, Connecticut

Main Gate (pages 102–105)
Pfizer U.S. Pharmaceuticals
Groton, Connecticut
Client: Pfizer U. S. Pharmaceuticals
Project Designers: Chad Floyd and James R. Martin
Project Team: Robert L. Harper, Darin C. Cook, Jonathan G. Parks, Steven E. Tiezzi, Paul Mellblom
Landscape Architect: Lester Collins with Anne Lacouture Penniman
Consulting Engineers: Besier Gibble Norden (structural), van Zelm Heywood & Shadford Inc. (mechanical, electrical), Radcliffe Engineering (civil)
Consultants: Colin Brash, Architectural Resources (CAD), Rumney Associates (graphics), Andrew Chartwell & Company (cost)
Contractor: Cutler Associates, Inc.

Technology Building (page 106)
Pfizer U.S. Pharmaceuticals
Groton, Connecticut
Client: Pfizer U. S. Pharmaceuticals
Project Designers: Chad Floyd and Nick Deaver
Project Team: Stephen B. Holmes, Peter T. Coffin, Edward J. Keagle, Michael J. Milne, Sheri Bryant Lucero, James A. Coan, Daniel H. Glynn, Darin C. Cook, John M. Doyle, George W. Penniman, Michelle R. LaFoe, James R. Martin, Sheryl A. Milardo
Consulting Engineers: Besier Gibble Norden (structural), van Zelm Heywood & Shadford, Inc. (mechanical, electrical)
Consultants: Andrew Chartwell & Company (cost)
Contractor: Pfizer, Incorporated

South Gate (page 107)
Pfizer U.S. Pharmaceuticals
Groton, Connecticut
Client: Pfizer U. S. Pharmaceuticals
Project Designers: Chad Floyd and Jean E. Smajstrla
Project Team: James R. Martin, George W. Penniman, Darin C. Cook, Howard A. Langner
Landscape Architects: Lester Collins and Anne Lacouture Penniman
Consulting Engineers: Besier Gibble Norden (structural), van Zelm Heywood & Shadford, Inc. (mechanical, electrical)
Consultants: Andrew Chartwell & Company (cost), Colin Brash, Architectural Resources (CAD)
Contractor: F.I.P. Construction, Inc.

Control Room (page 106)
Pfizer U.S. Pharmaceuticals
Groton, Connecticut
Client: Pfizer U. S. Pharmaceuticals
Project Designers: Chad Floyd and James R. Martin
Project Team: Paul C. Mellblom, Darin C. Cook
Consulting Engineers: van Zelm Heywood & Shadford Inc. (mechanical, electrical)
Contractor: F.I.P. Construction, Inc.

Gordon House (pages 108–109)
New England Coast
Client: Mr. and Mrs. Samuel L. Gordon
Project Designers: Mark Simon and Mahdad Saniee
Project Team: Steven E. Tiezzi, Stephen B. Holmes, Jonathan G. Parks
Landscape Architect: Lester Collins
Contractor: Richard Riggio & Sons

The Carl and Ruth Shapiro Admissions Center (pages 110–111)
Brandeis University
Waltham, Massachusetts
Client: Brandeis University
Project Designers: Mark Simon and Mahdad Saniee
Project Team: Michelle R. LaFoe, Sheryl A. Milardo, Darin C. Cook, Elizabeth A. DiSalvo, John M. Doyle
Landscape Architect: Morgan Wheelock
Furniture Design: Mark Simon
Consulting Engineers: Besier Gibble Norden (structural), Robert Van Houten, P.E. (mechanical, electrical), P. R. Sherman (code)
Contractor: Brandeis University/Twilight Construction

House in the Hudson Valley (pages 112–117)
Upstate New York
Project Designers: Jefferson B. Riley and Charles G. Mueller
Project Team: Steven E. Tiezzi, Robert G. Proctor, John M. Doyle, Sheryl A. Milardo
Landscape: Centerbrook and Lester Collins
Consulting Engineers: Besier Gibble Norden (structural), James E. Berning, P.E. (mechanical)
Contractor: Cal Parlman, Inc.

Rathskeller (pages 118–121)
    Quinnipiac College
    Hamden, Connecticut
    Client: Quinnipiac College
    Project Designers: Jefferson B. Riley and Leonard J. Wyeth
    Project Team: Roger U. Williams, Elizabeth A. DiSalvo, Sheri Bryant
    Lucero, Stephen B. Holmes, Jonathan G. Parks, J. Richard Staub, John
    Simonetti, Sheryl A. Milardo
    Landscape: Centerbrook with Michael Cegan, Richter Cegan & Webb
    Consulting Engineers: Besier Gibble Norden (structural),
    R. G. Vanderweil Engineers (mechanical, electrical), Nathan L. Jacobson
    & Associates (civil)
    Consultants: Systems Design Associates (lighting)
    Contractor: F. I. P. Construction Inc.

Pall Corporation Technical Center (pages 122–125)
    Port Washington, New York
    Client: Pall Corporation
    Project Designers: William H. Grover and Dennis J. Dowd
    Project Team: Walker J. Burns III, Steven E. Tiezzi, Susan E. Wyeth,
    Daniel H. Glynn, Roger U. Williams, C. Todd Delfosse, Stephen B.
    Holmes, John M. Doyle, Michael J. Milne, Jon M. Lavy, Sheryl A.
    Milardo, Jamison Cox
    Consulting Engineers: Besier Gibble Norden (structural),
    R. G. Vanderweil Engineers (mechanical, electrical), H2M Group (civil)
    Consultants: Chapman Ducibella Associates (security), Crabtree
    McGrath Associates, Inc. (food service), P. R. Sherman Inc. (code), Shen
    Milsom & Wilke (acoustics, audio-visual), Robert Schwartz & Associates
    (specifications), Ulshafer Associates (deionized water), Hoffmann
    Architects (roofing), Mario Designs (furnishings)
    Contractor: Turner Construction Company

Pall Corporation Headquarters (pages 126–129)
    East Hills, New York
    Client: Pall Corporation
    Project Designers: William H. Grover and Matthew C. Conley
    Project Team: Dennis J. Dowd, Jon M. Lavy, Susan E. Wyeth, Walker J.
    Burns III, Stephen B. Holmes, John M. Doyle, Matthew Johnson, Sheryl
    A. Milardo, J. Richard Staub, Liam Winters, Howard A. Langner, Robert
    L. Harper, Robert T. Coolidge, Evan Markiewicz, Daniel H. Glynn,
    Jonathan G. Parks, Michael J. Crosbie, Edward J. Keagle, Daniel M.
    Vickers, Michael J. Milne, John D. Kennedy, Robert G. Proctor, Ann L.
    Patterson, Michael Garner, Richard L. King, Steven E. Tiezzi
    Consulting Engineers: Besier Gibble Norden (structural),
    R. G. Vanderweil Engineers (mechanical)
    Consultants: Industrial and Environmental Analysts, Inc. (ultrapure
    water system)
    Contractor: Dominick Milone Inc.

Residence Hall (pages 130–133)
    Quinnipiac College
    Hamden, Connecticut
    Client: Quinnipiac College
    Project Designers: Jefferson B. Riley and Charles G. Mueller
    Project Team: Jonathan G. Parks, Michelle R. LaFoe, John M. Doyle,
    Charlotte C. Breed, Sheryl A. Milardo
    Consulting Engineers: Besier Gibble Norden (structural),
    R. G. Vanderweil Engineers (mechanical, electrical), Nathan L. Jacobson &
    Associates (civil, bridge)
    Consultants: Spec*Tran (specifications), Andrew Chartwell & Company (cost)
    Contractor: F.I.P. Construction, Inc.

House in Central Connecticut (pages 134–135)
    Project Designer: Robert L. Harper
    Project Managers: Charles G. Mueller and Christopher Arelt
    Landscape Architect: Richter Cegan & Webb
    Consulting Engineers: BVH Engineers Inc. (mechanical)
    Contractor: Liljedahl Brothers Inc.

Media Laboratory (pages 136–139)
    Massachusetts Institute of Technology
    Cambridge, Massachusetts
    Client: Massachusetts Institute of Technology
    Project Designers: Mark Simon with Mahdad Saniee
    Project Team: D. Michael Hellinghausen, Darin C. Cook, Peter T. Coffin,
    Sheryl A. Milardo, Julia Harrison, Paul L. Shainberg, Megan N. Gibson,
    Elizabeth A. DiSalvo, C. Todd Delfosse, Walker J. Burns III
    Consulting Engineers: Besier Gibble Norden (structural),
    R. G. Vanderweil Engineers (mechanical, electrical, plumbing)
    Consultants: P. R. Sherman (code), Systems Design Associates (lighting,
    theater)
    Contractor: Kennedy & Rossi

Western Maryland College (pages 140–143)
    Westminster, Maryland
    Client: Western Maryland College
    Project Designers: William H. Grover and James R. Martin
    Project Team for Clementine and Duane L. Peterson Fine Arts Building:
    Elizabeth A. DiSalvo, Gregory E. Nucci, Sheri Bryant Lucero, Liam Winters,
    Matthew C. Conley, Michelle R. LaFoe, Michael J. Milne
    Project Team for Hill Hall: Daniel H. Glynn, Jonathan G. Parks, Stephen B.
    Holmes, Sheri Bryant Lucero, Liam Winters, Matthew Johnson, Matthew C.
    Conley, Elizabeth A. DiSalvo, Michelle R. LaFoe, Gregory E. Nucci, George
    W. Penniman, David L. Huggins
    Project Team for Alumni Hall : Michelle R. LaFoe, Liam Winters, Elizabeth
    A. DiSalvo, Stephen B. Holmes, Sheri Bryant Lucero
    Project Team for The Studio: Elizabeth A. DiSalvo, Liam Winters,
    Stephen B. Holmes
    Landscape Architect: Design Group Inc.

Consulting Engineers: Besier Gibble Norden (structural), Gipe Associates (mechanical, electrical, plumbing), Whitney, Bailey, Cox & Magnani (civil)
Consultants: Andrew Chartwell & Company (cost)
Contractor: Roy Kirby and Sons, Construction Co.

Jones House (pages 144–145)
Greenwich, Connecticut
Client: Mr. and Mrs. Michael B. Jones
Project Designers: James C. Childress and Jon M. Lavy
Project Team: Liam Winters, Elizabeth A. DiSalvo
Contractor: Coburn Construction

Shaw's Cove Medical Arts Building (pages 146–147)
New London, Connecticut
Client: New London Medical Arts Group
Project Designers: William H. Grover and Gregory E. Nucci
Project Team: James A. Coan, Paul L. Shainberg
Consulting Engineers: Besier Gibble Norden (structural), van Zelm Heywood & Shadford Inc. (mechanical)
Contractor: F.I.P. Construction, Inc.

O'Connell House (pages 148–149)
Fairfield County, Connecticut
Client: Dr. Joseph B. O'Connell
Project Designer: Robert L. Harper
Project Team: Walker J. Burns III (project manager), Christopher Arelt
Contractor: W. R. T. Smith Builders, Inc.

School of Law Center (pages 150–159)
Quinnipiac College
Hamden, Connecticut
Client: Quinnipiac College
Project Designers: Jefferson B. Riley and James C. Childress
Project Team: C. Todd Delfosse, Ida Vorum, Michael Garner, Daniel H. Glynn, John M. Doyle, Peter T. Coffin, Christopher Arelt, J. Richard Staub, Liam Winters, Charles G. Mueller, Sheryl A. Milardo, Megan N. Gibson
Landscape: Centerbrook with Michael Cegan, Richter Cegan & Webb
Consulting Engineers: Besier Gibble Norden (structural), R. G. Vanderweil Engineers (mechanical, electrical, plumbing), Nathan L. Jacobson & Associates (civil)
Consultants: P. R. Sherman (code), Andrew Chartwell & Company (cost), Haley & Aldrich Inc. (geotechnical), Spec*Tran (specifications), Systems Design Associates (lighting), Klepper Marshall King Associates (acoustics), Chapman Ducibella Associates (security), Hans Knutzen Associates, Inc. (audio-visual), Vaughn Woodwork (millwork)
Contractor: Fusco Inc.

Food Science Research Laboratory (pages 160–163)
Pfizer Incorporated
Groton, Connecticut
Client: Pfizer Incorporated, Food Science Group
Project Designers: Chad Floyd and James A. Coan
Project Team: Edward J. Keagle, Darin C. Cook, Gregory E. Nucci

Landscape Architect: CUH2A
Consulting Engineers: Besier Gibble Norden (structural), van Zelm Heywood & Shadford, Inc. (mechanical, electrical), Radcliffe Engineering (civil)
Consultants: Verrex Inc. (teleconference), Andrew Chartwell & Company (cost), Robert Schwartz & Associates (specifications)
Contractor: C. R. Klewin Construction Co. Inc.

Urban Garden (pages 164–165)
Eastern United States
Project Designers: Mark Simon and James C. Childress
Project Team: Jon M. Lavy, Elizabeth A. DiSalvo, Matthew Johnson
Landscape Architect: Lester Collins
Consultants: Judith Mills-Johnson (horticulturist, landscape contractor)
Contractor: Meader Associates Inc.

Centennial Academic and Arts Center (pages 166–171)
Pomfret School
Pomfret, Connecticut
Client: Pomfret School
Project Designers: Mark Simon and Nick Deaver
Project Team: Peter T. Coffin, Mahdad Saniee, Sheri Bryant Lucero, Paul L. Shainberg, Darin C. Cook, Sheryl A. Milardo, Charlotte C. Breed, Jonas M. Goldberg, Robert L. Harper
Landscape: Maggie Daly
Consulting Engineers: Besier Gibble Norden (structural), BVH (civil, mechanical, electrical, plumbing)
Consultants: Systems Design Associates (lighting, theater), Andrew Chartwell & Company (cost)
Contractor: Inco/Larson Group

Pyne Dormitory (pages 166–171)
Pomfret School
Pomfret, Connecticut
Client: Pomfret School
Project Designers: Mark Simon with Paul L. Shainberg
Project Team: Nick Deaver, Sheri Bryant Lucero, Darin C. Cook, Sheryl A. Milardo, Robert L. Harper
Consulting Engineers: Besier Gibble Norden (structural), BVH (civil, mechanical, electrical, plumbing)
Consultants: Andrew Chartwell & Company (cost)
Contractor: Cutler Associates Inc.

Kitchings House (pages 172–173)
Essex, Connecticut
Client: Chester and Suzanne Kitchings
Project Designer: William H. Grover
Project Team: Charlotte C. Breed (project manager), Sheryl A. Milardo
Consulting Engineers: Besier Gibble Norden (structural), Acorn Consulting Engineers, Inc. (mechanical)
Contractor: A. J. Shea Construction

Guyott House (pages 174–181)
  Connecticut Coast
  Client: Mr. and Mrs. Francis R. Guyott, Jr.
  Project Designers: Mark Simon and Dennis Dowd
  Project Team: Darin C. Cook, Paul L. Shainberg, Steven E. Tiezzi,
  Elizabeth A. DiSalvo, Mahdad Saniee, Sheryl A. Milardo, Robert L.
  Harper, Megan N. Gibson, Edward J. Keagle
  Landscape Architect: Michael Van Valkenburgh, Associates Inc.
  Consulting Engineers: Besier Gibble Norden (structural), Robert Van
  Houten (mechanical), Thomas Metcalf (civil)
  Consultants: Bernard Burge (interiors), Richard Doerer (model maker),
  Andrew Chartwell & Company (cost), Margaret Wazuka (model
  photographer)
  Contractor: A. J. Shea Construction

Norton Museum of Art (pages 182–185)
  West Palm Beach, Florida
  Client: Norton Museum of Art
  Project Designer: Chad Floyd with Jean E. Smajstrla
  Project Team: Reno J. Migani, Jr., Jonathan G. Parks, Stephen B.
  Holmes, Walker J. Burns III, Matthew C. Conley, Roger U. Williams,
  Daniel H. Glynn, Peter T. Coffin, Megan N. Gibson, Sheryl A. Milardo
  Landscape Architect: Sanchez and Maddux Inc.
  Consulting Engineers: Besier Gibble Norden (structural), G. R. G.
  Vanderweil Engineers (mechanical, electrical, plumbing, fire protection),
  Shalloway, Foy, Rayman & Newell Inc. (civil)
  Consultants: P.R. Sherman Inc. (fire protection), Chapman Ducibella
  Associates (security), Systems Design Associates (lighting), Crabtree
  McGrath Associates Inc. (food service), Williamstown Art Conservation
  Center Inc. (conservation), Rumney Associates (graphics), Ardaman &
  Associates Inc. (soils), Robert Schwartz & Associates (specifications)
  Contractor: Suffolk Construction Co. Inc.

*A*uthor and Contributors

Andrea Oppenheimer Dean was for many years the executive editor of *Architecture* magazine. She is the author of *Bruno Zevi: On Modern Architecture,* the editor-at-large of *Preservation* magazine, a contributor to various design publications, and a Fellow of the American Academy in Rome.

Vincent J. Scully, Jr. teaches the history of architecture and urbanism at Yale University and the University of Miami. Professor Scully's many seminal books on subjects ranging from pueblos to Greek temples to modern architecture have made him America's most renowned architectural historian.

Nicholas Negroponte is the founder and director of the MIT Media Lab, where he holds the Wiesner Chair for Media Arts and Science. He is a founder of *WiReD* magazine and author of the best-seller *Being Digital.*